GAME FACE

Corporate Success Strategies of a Trail-Blazing Tech Warrior

VICKI WRIGHT-HAMILTON

GAME FACE:

Corporate Success Strategies of a

Trail-Blazing Tech Warrior

Published By: Vicki Wright-Hamilton

Roswell, GA 30076, USA

Editors:

Tashana Thompson | Beyond Business Solutions

Denise Renee Phinn | TheDerencoAgency

Book Cover & Interior Layout:

Nick F. Nelson | Brandprenuer

Tashana Thompson | Beyond Business Solutions

ISBN: 978-0-692-17417-3

Disclaimer:

In this personal account, the author has recreated events, locales and conversations from her memories of them. Some names and identifying details have been changed to protect the privacy of individuals and/or corporations.

DEDICATION

This book is dedicated, in the loving memory of my dear mother Dr. Irene Wright and my brother Tommy Wright.

Thank you for always encouraging me to tell my story. This one is for you.

Acknowledgments

I am forever indebted to my incredible parents, Drs. Thomas & Irene Wright, because of them, I AM. Mom and Dad thank you for always being such wonderful role models. You set the foundation that has propelled my life forward. Mama thank you for reminding me of the reason that I had to share this work with the world "to serve others".

To my husband, Harold thank you for always supporting me, your love and partnership make the difference in my life. You have led by example and shown our sons what a "real man" looks like. To my oldest son, Arthur thank you for your unconditional love, being my cheerleader on this journey. You have such an amazing heart, thank you for being such an amazing big brother as well. To my daughter-in-law, Angelica, for always being there and your willingness to help. To my youngest son, Brandon, thank you for helping me to believe in the power of my story. Last, but certainly not least, to my grandson Armando Jay, I hope my story helps you to learn a bit more about your Vivi.

I am also grateful for my friends and colleagues that have become my extended family. Thank you to my awesome network at VPAK for giving me the encouragement and accountability I needed to complete this book. Many thanks to my business and marketing consultant Tashana Thompson, for all of her assistance and brutal honesty.

TABLE OF CONTENTS

Acknowledgments v

Introduction 1

Chapter 1: Game Face Boot Camp 5

Chapter 2: Wright Family Values 9

Chapter 3: The Ultimate Sacrifice 17

Chapter 4: Good Girls Get Picked For Great Jobs First 29

Chapter 5: Cold Days In Minnesota 37

Chapter 6: Pregnancy, Promotion, And A Vision From God 45

Chapter 7: Diary Of A Successful Black Single Mother 55

Chapter 8: Bad Things Happen To Good People 67

Chapter 9: Back To Love, Back To School 81

Chapter 10: Will My Real Husband Please Stand Up? 89

Chapter 11: The Leader I Always Wanted To Have 99

Chapter 12: Adventures In Diversity 113

Chapter 13: Actions Speak Louder Than Words 129

Chapter 14: Learning Different Leadership Styles 139

Chapter 15: The Accidental Entrepreneur 149

Chapter 16: Caring For Family, Caring For Self........................... 163

Introduction

Dear Reader,

Thank you! I am beyond grateful and so humbled that you are taking the time to read this book. Within these pages, you will find many of the triumphs and defeats I have experienced throughout my corporate career and over my decades of life experience.

I want you to understand what I mean by the term "Game Face." There are many times we may find it necessary to shield our "authentic feelings." We might put on a "game face" so we can protect ourselves from embarrassment or ridicule. Other times, our game face might be necessary to help us keep moving forward through a challenging situation. We put on game faces as a survival mechanism in both our personal and professional lives.

For some people, their game face is having a tough exterior. My personal game face is a big smile. I learned early in life that the easiest way for me to get along with everyone and get through my tough and disappointing situations was to be as pleasant as possible and go with the flow even if I disagreed with the direction things were going in. I learned early in life to put the greater good of the whole before my own feelings or desires. If I put a big smile on my face and seemed to go with the flow, then people around me thought I was ok. So, it shifted their attention away from me, which gave me the mental space to sort out my feelings and force them to catch up with my "greater good" decision.

I've shared with you mine; what's your game face? I'm sure you know from your own personal experience that having a game face is tough. It is hard to feel like we always need to protect ourselves emotionally. If we use our game faces too much, we can easily go down the slippery slope of pretending to be someone we are not. The inability to communicate and express our authentic feelings can create toxic people and environments. Stifling our feelings can become strenuous on the mind, body, and soul. If we've reached that point, we are no good to anyone, least of all, ourselves.

However, managed correctly, a game face can help you power through and come out successful on the other side. My game face has served me well in my career as you will come to see in the stories I share throughout this book. I am blessed by the opportunities I've had in my career. I rose to executive level positions as a black woman in the predominantly white male world of technology. I hope that my story will let you know you are not alone. You can wear your game face when it is necessary. You can also express and communicate your authentic emotions. This will bring you into your true success in all areas of your life. As you dive into my story, I pray it encourages you.

CHAPTER 1

Game Face Boot Camp

My family life was my first training ground for my game face. I guess you can call it "boot camp." And not just because my father was in the military or because I was an Air Force brat. I learned very early in my life that to be successful in my career and personal relationships, I needed to pause certain emotions I felt and show I was ok with being a team player. I learned early on that I needed to adapt to situations. But before I get too far ahead of myself, let me set the scene for you.

I was born in 1963 as the youngest child of Dr. Thomas and Dr. Irene Wright. Both my parents came from very humble beginnings. Being born Black in the 1920's and 1930's in America, their only hope for rising above would be through hard work and education. My mother was the Dean of Students at Albany State College in Georgia. Her career was well on its way when she met my father. The Air Force had him stationed in Albany, Georgia. The two fell in love, married and immediately had children. I have two older sisters, Marcia and Lynn, and my brother Tommy is next in line. I am the "baby" so I'm sure you can imagine the childhood full of compromises and situations where I didn't get my way that lay ahead of me.

One of my earliest lessons in adapting to situations and learning to have a smiling public face happened when I was around five years old. My dad was stationed in Okinawa, Japan and we lived there with him for several years. There was an annual celebration planned to honor the sacrifice of fallen soldiers. They selected a boy and a girl to be Poppy King and Queen. The King and Queen took part in the festivities. The selection process was rigorous and there were strict requirements for participation. When they announced I would be Poppy Queen, I felt honored. My responsibilities included giving speeches, making television appearances, meeting with commissioned officers, and distinguished photo ops. It was my job to always have a pretty smile on my face for every event. I credit this experience for giving me the confidence to speak in public.

I enjoyed being a military brat. We moved often. Every few years, we got to live in a different place. I loved being exposed to and learning about different cultures. At a young age, diversity fueled me. But military life ended because my father made a major decision to take a stand for himself.

Daddy was a commissioned officer and had an exemplary record. Hard work was one of his core values. But his superior officers denied him a promotion twice. In those days, during the 1960s, the United States military did not promote black men. Especially not bold, courageous black men like my Civil Rights championing father.

My mother and father were active in the Civil Rights movement. They were among the founding members of the Albany movement. They met and marched alongside the pioneers: Dr. Martin Luther King, Andrew Young, Bernard Lee, and many others. Several of those legends were guests in our home.

My parents are firm believers in standing up for whatever they believed was right. They risked career advancement for the betterment of their family. My parents were adamant about ensuring their children had the same opportunities as any other American child. Their early example taught me not to be afraid of doing the right thing even if the right thing came with negative consequences.

My fathers' belief in the principles of the Civil Rights movement brought his otherwise shining Air Force career to a screeching halt. He was being blocked from any further advancement because of the color of his skin. He decided to leave the military. But on his way out, he took advantage of his G.I. Bill benefits and pursued his education. He completed his bachelor's degree in 1969. He went on to earn a master's degree and finished his Ph.D. studies in 1978. Wow! What an accomplishment! Better still, he modeled everything he had been teaching us kids; education was the key to advancement and success.

But there were other lessons I learned. While my father was in school, my mother worked diligently to support our family's financial necessities. I saw sacrifice and compromise modeled as my parents worked towards the greater good of improving the family. Soon, I experienced for myself what sacrifice and compromising was all about, and I got more opportunities to use my game face.

CHAPTER 2

Wright Family Values

While I liked the military lifestyle, there were downsides. The most significant one is that I never felt as though I had a real home. To this day, when my friends talk about where they are from and how they grew up with the same group of friends, I can't relate to their experiences.

Even though my parents owned homes during our military years, we were never in one place for too long. So, when my parents settled in Los Angeles, California after my father exited the Service, I was excited. I thought that our family would be there long-term, but it was just a stopping point. I was finally in a neighborhood I could call home. But my new sense of "home" was short-lived. We moved ten months later to University City, a suburb of St. Louis, Missouri. My father's new career caused us to move just as frequently as the military had.

Constantly moving in my early years taught me how to adapt quickly to new situations. I never knew when I had to pack my bags and head off to a new neighborhood and school. So, I learned to put a big smile on my face and make new friends fast. I grew to have a healthy love of change. The experience shaped an area of my personality; I now get bored quickly when things stay the same for too long. Change fuels me. It became an important driver throughout my career as you'll soon see in future chapters.

If there was any "superpower" I possessed as a child, I would say it was my power of observation. It kept me out of trouble and got me what I wanted. My parents, but particularly my father, were strict. I never wanted to see my dad get upset, neither did I want to get in trouble with him. My older siblings, not so much. Every time they got in trouble, I made a mental note. Whatever mistakes they made, I was determined not to repeat them. I did not want to endure the punishments they received.

The benefit of being the baby was that I could see what my parents rewarded. The more I followed the rules, the more privileges I earned. My sisters would always call me spoiled because I often got whatever I wanted. I wasn't spoiled, I was smart. Blame it on my superpower!

Even though I knew the formula to getting what I wanted, it only worked to a certain extent. As the baby of the family I had to wait a long time before I could do what my older siblings did, like go to parties and hang out at a friend's house. I remember being jealous when Marcia and Lynn dated, and I couldn't. So, I figured if I couldn't have fun, they shouldn't either!

When I was around 8 or 9 years old, Lynn got to have guys come to our house to see her. I would go in the living room and plop myself between them with the biggest grin on my face! The guys would always say, "Your little sister is so cute!" That always brightened my day because that meant they loved seeing me. Lynn didn't share their sentiment.

Lynn would scream at the top of her lungs, "Mama, can you get Vicki!" I can't say my parents were too quick to put a stop to my antics. Whenever Dad was home, he loved me being the third wheel on their dates. He knew there would be no "funny business" if I was around to be a disruptive nuisance. But eventually, I was forced to leave and let my sister enjoy her company. But then not long after that, it was suddenly time for the male friend to leave. As I got older, I eventually stopped ruining their dates… but it was fun while it lasted!

My brother Tommy and I were only fourteen months apart. Being so close in age, he was my best friend, and we did everything together. But he was very much a boy! Tommy loved to prank and scare me. He often put plastic bugs and fake spiders in my bed. I would always scream my head off and have a fit; he doubled over with laughter every single time. I was his personal amusement!

In our household, the girls received a disproportionate amount of the chores. My brother was a "man", so he rarely did household chores. I had a long list of things to do: wash dishes, clean the bathroom, and vacuum. Meanwhile, Tommy only had to take out the trash and care for the dog. Yep. That's all! Occasionally he might help in the yard.

As the only boy in the family, Tommy received special treatment. For example, as we grew older, my parents allowed him to stay out later than I could. Seeing the disparities at home taught me early on that men and women were regarded differently. Tommy's special privileges bothered me, but I had to put on my game face every time my parents wouldn't allow me to do something Tommy could do. Despite it all, I still loved Tommy and cherished my close relationship with him.

There is one area, though, where everyone in my household was on an equal footing. Education. Excelling in school was mandatory for everyone, parents and children alike. We all had to work towards excellence in our professional careers. My parents definitely modeled that for us kids. And I appreciated knowing my gender would never be a hindrance in school or beyond. I knew early on that being a girl didn't stop me from performing well academically or meeting any goals I set.

Another value instilled in me was the importance of supporting your family. During the nine years my father was working on his collection of degrees, my mother worked her tail off to make sure that the family not only survived but thrived. She was a Dean at a college and her income paid the bills and kept us fed. She always taught us you do whatever is necessary to make things happen and move your family forward.

I often wondered how she felt carrying the financial burden by herself. Did she ever get tired or want to stop? Because I never once saw or heard my mother complain. Today when I reflect on that time period, I realize that my mom had her own game face on. She was adapting to her reality and did what she felt she had to do. If she and Daddy had any conflicts regarding this, I never knew about it. Observing my Mom shaped my sense of motherhood. I learned what it truly meant to sacrifice and make compromises for your family. And now, having my own family, I know firsthand that she put in a lot of hard work!

All the hard work paid off. My father had many graduation ceremonies and my entire family attended every single one. I adore my Dad and often wondered how he had the patience to make it through. How did he bounce back from being discriminated against in the Air Force? What gave him the confidence and drive to stick with his aggressive education plan? When I asked him recently, Daddy told me:

"When you want something, you will go after it. You must decide what is important to you. I wanted to give my family a great life and knew I needed my education to provide the best foundation for all of you. I am just thankful that your mother supported me during this time. I had to finish what I started."

As an adult looking back, I know my Dad had his own game face and used it to push past the barriers in his way. He felt hurt that the military disrespected and disregarded him repeatedly after he sacrificed so much for his country. Dad recently admitted he felt overwhelmed but could not let his children see that. He wanted us to see that hard work could pay off for anyone, regardless of their skin color. He didn't want us to know about the worry or stress he was facing emotionally. I appreciate and honor my Dad and my Mom for their dedication and examples. I learned from them it is never too late to learn, grow, or change the direction of your life.

CHAPTER 3

The Ultimate Sacrifice

Daddy finished his Ph.D. in Finance in 1979 when I was 16 years old. With those intense years completed, I thought our family life would settle down. Nope! Mama decided she wanted to earn her Ph.D.!

Mama already had her bachelor's from Spelman College, an HBCU (Historically Black Colleges and Universities) in Atlanta, Georgia. She had earned her master's from Atlanta University Center, now known as AUC Consortium. Now, she planned on pursuing her Ph.D. at Washington University in St. Louis, Missouri. But we lived in Dayton, Ohio which is two states and almost six hours away. That meant she would travel to attend classes and wouldn't be home during the week.

I instantly wondered what sacrifices the family needed to make this time around. How would we survive with Mama traveling all the time? Well, trust and believe she had a plan! We all needed to step up to the plate and do more to help in her absence. Cooking and keeping the house clean were my responsibilities.

With Mama away at school, Daddy decided he needed a new goal to pursue. Now was the perfect time for him to focus on shaving 35 pounds off his frame. I wondered what I would prepare for him since cooking was my task. But I was more worried about his mood. Would I be able to deal with him getting hungry and "evil" when I denied him his favorite foods?

But he had a prescribed meal plan, and I followed it to the letter. If it said oranges, I would hand him an orange. He would ask me, "Well, aren't you going to peel it or cut it in slices to at least make it look appetizing for me?" To which I replied, "An orange is an orange so here you go!" I didn't go through anything extra to make his diet food appear more appetizing. I thought you eat what is on the list. Any extra fluff takes too much time. I had other things to do! This became a joke between us we laugh about now. The good news is that Daddy lost the weight. My dinner service skills helped him reach his goal.

Occasionally, I would go to St. Louis with my mother. I often sat in her statistics courses and took notes for her. I loved math, so I was thrilled. I felt grown up because I was hanging out with adults at college. Mama's classmates nicknamed me the "little one."

Mama also allowed me to collect her data on computer cards, and that was awesome! I thought working with the computer cards was the greatest thing in the world. I even helped Mama type the rough drafts of her dissertation. The typewriter fascinated me. I was enamored by how the words appeared on the sheet of paper. Mama let me have my fun with it because she got free labor!

Helping my mom with her schooling and my dad with his weight loss were some of the fun times I had during my teen years. But my high school experiences weren't always so fun. My classmates always considered me to be "pleasantly plump" compared to a lot of the other petite girls around me. Everyone thought they had great bodies. As a result, I wasn't comfortable in my own skin.

I wanted to exercise and be with my peers, so I joined the cheerleading squad. Unfortunately, I was the largest one on the team. I didn't quite get the acceptance I was looking for. Even worse was my dating life. I had finally reached the age where I could date. But unlike Marcia and Lynn before me, I had no suitors who wanted to come to my home and sit on my couch to spend time with me.

This was devasting to my self-esteem. I had several male friends, and I often shared my feelings with them. I was the girl in the friend zone. I was good enough to talk to, but not to date. My friends told me I was the girl they would take home to their moms when they were ready to get married. But they were too young for that. For now, they wanted girls they could "have fun" with.

They were trying to make me feel better, but their words had the opposite effect. Really? I wasn't the girl to "have fun" with? My wholesome upbringing had branded me a "good girl" and that perception was hard to change. My friend's revelation hurt me. The rejection was too painful, but I wanted no one to know it bothered me. So, I put on my game face and focused on the one thing I knew no one could ever deny me: how smart I was. I put all my energy into making top grades. I pretended to be so into my studies I didn't have time for boys. To the outside world, I was unbothered by not having a boyfriend.

While in high school, I took a course to learn how to be a proof operator. In the late 1970s and early 80s, an NCR machine encoded the amount on checks. Since I loved computer cards and typing, I thought I should learn this trade. I figured if nothing else, I could always work in a bank as a proof operator. Since I didn't have boys vying for my attention, I had plenty of time to think about preparing for having a career!

Additionally, I took math classes at the local University during my senior year. I also completed the maximum amount of AP math courses I could. My game face was definitely on and I had a career strategy by the time I turned 18. I planned on being a proof operator and a math tutor. My goal was to work and be able to provide for myself. Success was in my sights. I did not want all my dateless nights and loneliness go to waste. "I will be somebody," I encouraged myself.

Like most high school seniors, I had anxieties about getting into college. I knew I had to take the SATs and ACTs for college admissions. I hated these standardized tests and never did well on them. Although I studied hard and made good grades, I always froze on these types of tests. They were so stressful. I had convinced myself that some people excelled at taking standardized tests; I wasn't one. I was afraid that if I didn't do well, I wouldn't be able to go to my dream school.

The only school I wanted to apply to, and attend was Spelman College, my Mama's alma mater. It's where she had been Dean of Women. Marcia and Lynn went to Spelman. My brother was in his freshman year at Morehouse College right across the street. The

Atlanta University Center schools were a family tradition, and I wasn't planning on breaking it.

During my senior year, I planned on taking part in the Alpha Kappa Alpha (AKA) Cotillion. At the Cotillion, they would announce which college I would be attending. So, I knew I needed to buckle down and do everything I could to make sure I wasn't embarrassed; I had to get into Spelman. I took my SATs and ACTs on their first available testing date.

One afternoon, I was in my room jamming to some music with my dog. Mama walked in.

"You have mail," she announced.

I froze in panic. "Is it from Spelman?" I asked.

"Yes," she said.

I was so terrified that I didn't even want her to open the letter. In her wisdom, my mother reminded me I needed to know in case I needed to develop a backup plan. I was so nervous that I was shaking and even started to tear up. Then, I couldn't stand it anymore.

"Ok, go ahead, open it!" I exclaimed.

Mama opened the letter and read silently. Tears flowed down her face. Oh no, I didn't make it! My heart sank.

But then she gathered herself and read the letter aloud. The first line told me she was crying tears of joy; they accepted me! But even better than being accepted, I was invited to be part of an exclusive pre-freshman program on campus that included a partial two-year scholarship.

I screamed! Now I had my own tears of joy! I cried and hugged my mother so tight. There was no containing my excitement. Now I could make my announcement at my upcoming Cotillion. My joy of going to Spelman overshadowed the fact that I was dateless for my Cotillion and prom. I didn't mind that Tommy flew home from Morehouse to rescue me. At least I would be spending an evening with someone I liked.

I had an amazing time at my Cotillion. I received another scholarship that evening. While my scholarships didn't fully cover all my college expenses, I knew if I worked hard, I didn't have to have significant debt after college. I determined that once I got to Spelman, I wasn't leaving. My closest cousin was already attending, and I knew we would be like white on rice! I was on top of the world! My hard work had made my biggest dream in life come true. I knew everything would be perfect.

I enrolled at Spelman College in 1981 as a computer science major. My major was a cooperative program between Spelman and Morehouse. All the classes were taught at Morehouse. In case you don't know, Spelman is an all-female college and Morehouse is all men. Few girls majored in computer science at that time. So, you can imagine my joy at often being the only girl in a classroom full of yummy, chocolate eye-candy! But don't get it twisted. I was focused! I always wanted to outshine my male counterparts. My professors would make comments to instigate and fuel this rivalry. I reveled in the competition; it prepared me to excel in a male-dominated industry.

The only downside to being at my dream college was that I worked multiple jobs all the time. I didn't have a lot of time to party and have fun between studying and working. I had decided I would be a successful career woman, so it meant I had to prioritize. Once again, I put on my game face. To my peers, I was a focused and dedicated student who didn't have time for frivolities. But deep down, I wanted to be partying with everyone else. Dating a fine "Morehouse Man" would have been nice too.

Even though I excelled at school, it didn't come easy for me. I worked hard to earn my good grades. To cushion the sting of not being able to have the typical fun-filled college experience, I moved off campus into an apartment during my second year. Not working was now not optional; I had to pay my own bills. My parents told me they would not contribute. I was fine with our agreement because I still loved my life at my dream school.

When I look back on this period of my life, I wish I had given myself the opportunity to have a little more fun than I did. Still, I enjoyed my time at Spelman tremendously, especially because I shared it with my close cousin. She made everything that much better. We spent all our none working hours hanging out together. But it all came to an end.

As I neared the end of my sophomore year at Spelman, my parents revealed that they were not happy about me spending late nights waiting in the computer lab. They had a "brilliant" plan to alleviate that need. Daddy now worked at The University of Dayton. The university was beginning their first class of a new Management Information Systems degree program. If I transferred schools, I could be a member of the program's first graduating class. Better still, I could take advantage of Daddy's benefits and complete my education for free. Living at home for free was a given. I wouldn't have to work; I could just focus on studying.

Not having to work sounded nice. The thought of a free education was compelling too, but I wasn't interested in leaving Spelman. Besides, the whole point of college was to be away from home! If I went back, I would be living in my own personal hell. Not only would I see Daddy at home, but my classes would be in the same building where he worked. He would be all over me about my classes and grades! I hated this idea! I asked my father if we could talk more about it later, but he emphasized that I would have to apply for admission immediately. To keep the peace, I applied. To no one's surprise, they accepted me.

It meant a lot to me that I could go to school without causing my parents or myself any financial stress. Their argument made sense, and I didn't want to be selfish. The decision was a sound financial benefit for the family. But leaving Spelman made me feel as though I had failed. I had only partially completed my dream. I had gotten into the school, but I wouldn't be finishing my degree there. I wanted to be like my mother, sisters, and other relatives who had graduated from an Atlanta University Center school.

I called my mother and wept uncontrollably. Mama tried her best to console me. "Once a Spelmanite, always a Spelmanite," she said. "You are still a part of the family legacy. You attended for two and a half years. No one can take that away from you."

I appreciated her words of encouragement, but I wasn't looking forward to going to a new school. It was not an HBCU; that is the college experience I wanted. In the end, I put on my game face and did what was best for my family and my financial future, even if it wasn't what I truly wanted. It pained me to sacrifice my biggest dream in life up to that point.

CHAPTER 4

Good Girls Get Picked for Great Jobs First

When I arrived at the University of Dayton, my attitude was, "I am just here to get an education." I didn't like this school. I didn't choose this school. I wasn't there to make friends. My cousin wasn't with me. I had none of my familiar support system around me. All I had was my dad. Whoopee!

Most people on campus didn't know my father was part of the faculty, and I tried my best to keep it that way. I kept my head down. I went to class, then to work. Constantly working was my excuse for not being social on campus.

My parents didn't bother me about working unnecessarily. The thought of working was "my thing" and figured the experience would only help me once I graduated. However, the truth was I worked to keep myself busy. It was my way of hiding how miserable I was. I didn't want to seem ungrateful to my parents by telling them how I really felt. So, I kept my game face on and powered through. Whenever I was home, I would stay in my room, play music, and dance my heart out to keep from crying. After a vigorous dance session, I would study until early morning hours.

While at the University of Dayton, I had an experience I will never forget. Early in the semester, I took a test for my business technology course and received a D as my grade. It did not reflect how much I had studied. By the school standards, I had failed the exam. My professor made a 'B-Line' down to my father's office to tell him I failed the test. He said to my father he wasn't sure I was in the right major.

That night at dinner Daddy said,

"Vicki, I understand that you failed a test today. What happened?"

I was horrified. This is exactly what I had feared would happen. I couldn't avoid him or the conversation.

"Yes, I failed," I admitted. "I don't know what happened. I worked very hard on studying the material." I gave him my plan of action to rectify the situation. First, I would meet with my professor to understand my mistakes. Then, I would attend study sessions to get extra help.

My father then asked me,

"Are you sure this is what you want to do? Your professor thinks this might not be the right major for you."

Why did Daddy say that in front of Mama? Boy did the sparks and anger fly! Mama jumped in before I could speak. She let him know no man would determine her child's future because of one bad test. After putting Daddy in his place, she focused her intensity on me and told me to go get my books. My study sessions would start immediately.

I felt horrible. I cried my eyes out. I didn't like being the source of Mama and Daddy arguing. Plus, I had never failed at anything academically in my life. Working hard had always paid off for me. But this time I came up short.

The next day, I visited my professor as planned. He told me to my face what he said to my Dad.

"Vicki, I just don't think you are in the right major. You should really change it now before it gets too late."

Something inside me snapped. I looked at him. "I am not changing anything!" I said. "I will succeed and make it through this class!" I stormed out of his office.

Although I had given my professor a steely stare, my best game face, and showed my gritty determination, the truth is my confidence had taken a tremendous hit. I needed not only academic help but emotional support. Thank God for Mama! She was my biggest cheerleader and study coach. She kept reminding me of my strengths and talents. She would not let me focus on my professor's opinion of me. I listened to her and did everything she told me to do.

Mama was a drill sergeant. I worked hard before but now it was on another level. She frequently quizzed me. She often made me explain my answers orally to ensure I understood the concepts. The hard work paid off. I passed the class with a B-. I was so happy about it, you would have thought it was an A+!

Challenges cause us to grow more than when things are going smoothly. One thing I appreciate about my struggle with this class is that as a result, I gained more efficient study habits. It restored my faith in hard work; this situation taught me that sometimes you have to dig a little deeper to come out with the win.

Even though I passed the class, my professor's words stayed with me for a long time. As it so happens, his class was the only one in my major I ever had a problem with. So, as I continued taking my courses, it became easier to take back my power and prove to myself that I belonged in the rigorous major.

With graduation fast approaching, I became anxious about adult pressures and the next chapter of my life. Where would I work? Who will give me my first job in my career? I was the queen of working all throughout college. Now I worried about not getting interviews or job offers when it really counted. I knew being a girl and an African American graduating with a computer science degree, I would face stiff competition. I wasn't sure if I would really get a job.

Thankfully, the University of Dayton had a great career center on campus. I attended every event and program offered. I took advantage of anything that could help me with my future. I sacrificed a lot of Saturday afternoons by attending events and volunteering. Because of being connected to the career center, I learned about opportunities first. I interviewed with many companies. I hoped at least one opportunity would come through.

I was home one Thursday morning when the phone rang. It was a representative from a company I interviewed with, AzTech Global (names of all companies have been changed). They were calling to make me an offer. I was so thrilled, I couldn't wipe the grin off my face as I spoke with the representative.

While we still talked, I heard a chiming tone. It was the new call-waiting feature on our phone. I respectfully asked if they could hold the line while I answered; I assumed it was a call for one of my parents. You could have knocked me over with a feather when I discovered it was yet another company, NutriCorp, from my slew of interviews. They, too, were calling to extend a job offer.

I couldn't have dreamed up this scenario in my wildest imagination! I listened to their offer and then asked them to hold just a moment. I clicked back over and told AzTech Global (AG) that I genuinely appreciated their offer, but I had received another offer and wanted to go with it. To my delightful surprise, an AG representative countered the NutriCorp offer! So, I asked them to hold on. I clicked back over and told the NutriCorp representative that although I was very interested, I planned to accept the AG offer. NutriCorp was persistent. They increased their offer and added a few other perks. It was too good to refuse. So, I clicked back over to AzTech Global and ended the conversation with them. They told me if I changed my mind to please call them back.

I was on top of the world! Two companies wanted me to work for them and they proved it by fighting for me! I might not have been the girl guys wanted to have fun with, but I sure was the girl companies wanted to hire! Being a good girl finally paid off when it mattered most… literally!

NutriCorp is a large food company based in Minnesota. Their programs for recent graduates were excellent and well known. My father was beyond delighted to hear about the multiple job opportunities they had offered his baby girl. He said, "I have never seen anyone get over a 20% raise in 15 min!"

The experience taught me right at the beginning of my career that negotiating is extremely important. I might need a job, but the hiring company needs my skills. If they truly want me, I needed to make them work to get me. They will make an attractive offer as long as I negotiate for it.

This was a great way to cap off my time at the University of Dayton. The highlight of my experience at the school came on graduation day. When I walked across the stage to get my degree, guess who had the honor of handing it to me? Daddy gave me my degree along with the biggest bear hug. That day, I didn't care who knew he was my father. It was a proud and special moment for both of us.

CHAPTER 5

Cold Days in Minnesota

Just weeks after graduation, I moved to Minneapolis, Minnesota in June 1985. This was the real world. I had nothing and no one familiar to rely on. It differed from when I had my apartment at Spelman. I was now solely responsible for caring for myself and building my life.

To say I was not a fan of Minneapolis weather would be putting it mildly. I experienced cold on another level. One year, it snowed in May! I never spent a Memorial Day without barbequing, except that year! Since I hated the cold weather, I stayed indoors and hibernated. Frankly, I hibernated all the time.

One of Minnesotan's favorite forms of entertainment is ice fishing. I received many invitations to go out to the lake. I thought, "You must be kidding! I am not going on any lake to sit in a hut and fish with a heater that can melt the ice and make me fall in!" But my friends finally wore me down; I tagged along once, just to say I did it. And just when the cold wore down my last nerve, the weather shifted from winter to mosquito season, just like that! There was no in between.

There were many days while I lived in Minnesota that I said to myself, "I can't do this!" Still, I stuck with the choice I made. I had fun times with the friends I met there. I learned firsthand how to make lemonade out of lemons when things don't go as expected.

But Minnesota wasn't all bad. I had a little sweetener for my lemonade. Remember back in high school, I was always in the friend zone with a few guys? Well, there was one I was a little friendlier with. I'll call him John.

John and I liked each other, but we headed in different directions for college. We promised to reconnect after school and explore if our relationship was "meant to be." Since neither of us made any serious romantic connections in college, we connected after graduation. Unfortunately, John didn't land a job immediately in his career after school. So, he eventually moved to Minnesota to be with me.

Once he got to Minneapolis, I tapped into my network to help him find a job. I worked with a lot of vendors at NutriCorp, so I started with them. My contacts introduced me to other businesses and connections that could assist John in his job search. I also reached out to people in my church for help. After my extensive networking, John found a job he enjoyed. I liked having John with me. Our relationship was the touch of warmth I needed during the cold Minnesota winters and the sometimes-chilly environment on my job.

I was initially hired at NutriCorp as a computer programmer. But within a year, I received a promotion to systems analyst. I created a brand-new operations department for an entire business unit. I had a lot of fun building a team from the ground up.

I was excited about the rapid success and the great opportunities I earned so quickly in my career. I reflected on my professor's harsh words; what if I had listened to him and quit my major? I guess I had shown him and myself how well what hard work and dedication paid off. And then, I had an idea. My professor had no clue what was happening in my career. So, I figured I'd tell him.

I made a copy of my paycheck (which I knew was more than his salary) and composed a simple note:

Dear Professor,

I hope that this note finds you well. I wanted to show you what "not being successful" really looks like.

Take care.

Vicki Wright

That felt so good, let me tell you! I kept him updated as my career progressed. After my next promotion, I sent him another letter. Yes, my motives were totally immature, but reminding myself of his lack of belief in my ability fueled me. It served as a personal reminder that no one had the power to define me or dictate what I can or cannot do.

I jumped feet first into my new role and department. My new boss was one of a few females in management. According to her management style, everything required her approval and her solutions were the best, regardless of your experiences or thoughts. Initially, I wanted to learn from her as much as I could. Boy, did I learn! I learned what kind of leader I did not want to be.

One day, she called my name and snapped her fingers at me. That rubbed me the wrong way. Automatically, I walked over to her and before I could censor myself, I said,

"Who are you calling? Surely it is not me. I am not your dog. You will not disrespect me!"

"Yes, I am talking to you," she replied. "I am the captain of this ship, and you are just riding on it!"

I thought to myself "This woman is crazy!" Yes, I needed a job, but she didn't have the right to treat me like trash. My parents fought too hard as Civil Rights activists and through their personal sacrifices for me to understand that I am a human being and deserved a certain amount of respect and dignity. I was hurt and, frankly, stunned that a leader would behave that way. A colleague witnessed the incident and suggested I talk to HR. Initially, I feared going to HR; I didn't think they would listen to or believe me. I worried about the outcomes. Ultimately, anger marched my feet into the HR office.

I had a good relationship with one of the HR executives. I recounted the incident to him. He looked at me oddly. He then said,

"Thanks for telling me. I will handle this. I will talk to your colleague and your boss."

You would think with an investigation into her behavior, my boss would have been more careful with how she acted. Nope. She continued to show her colors. In meetings, she purposefully discredited everything I said. I kept my game face on around her. I was smiling and pleasant on the outside, but on the inside, I was holding my breath. I never knew how she would act toward me.

My only comfort was in knowing the teams I supported loved me. I had built a great reputation with everyone. They always invited me to come to their areas and share my knowledge. I became an expert in the IBM AS/400 environment. Other departments around the company sought me out because of my expertise and ability. Vendors also requested that I consult with them.

Finally, the investigation period ended. HR asked to see me. They told me they had been receiving several complaints about my boss and that she would be out of the office for a while. I would now report to her boss directly. I was relieved but uneasy. I didn't know if she would return or what would happen when if she did. Thankfully, I never found out. After her time off, they dismissed her. This situation taught me a profound lesson about how to treat the people who work for you. We don't have the right to disrespect or mistreat anyone. I appreciated that the leadership at NutriCorp took everyone's feedback about this woman seriously and supported us.

I remained somewhat guarded after that experience, but I still loved my work. It was challenging, and I was creating a great department. I knew my clients and colleagues appreciated my efforts as everyone always asked for my opinions and support. That made me very happy. But I still had a lot to learn about leadership in the corporate world and boy was I about to receive a huge lesson.

Christmas was coming up. It is an important holiday for my family so naturally, I wanted to go home and spend time with them. I requested my vacation days. My superiors denied it. Once again, I had an "Are you kidding me?" moment. I had plenty of time accrued. I worked hard. I deserved to be with my family. My emotions ran wild. I already made a lot of personal sacrifices when I took the job in Minnesota. I worked constantly and gave them 200%. Now I had to give up more? "Is this what it takes to be successful," I asked myself.

The level of commitment required of you when you are leading a team is what I did not understand at the time. We had a major project launching. They denied my time off because they expected me to be present to manage my portion. I could not go home just because I wanted to. They needed me to get this project done, and I had to be there and make it happen.

It upset me that I couldn't be with my family, so I questioned my decision to be at NutriCorp. They expected me to give up a lot to work for them, but what did I get out of it? Well, of course, the answer was my comfortable paycheck and my health benefits. I didn't want to risk my job by displaying my true emotions. I had to put my game face on, smile, and go with the flow. If I was going to continue accepting their checks twice a month, then I needed to embrace my role and responsibilities fully and be grateful to have a job.

This early lesson in the expectations for corporate leaders benefited the rest of my career. I had sacrificed a lot of fun and frivolities in college in order to get great grades and to have a great career. Now advancing in that career required even more personal sacrifices. When you manage a major project, the deadlines for your deliverables may not happen on convenient days. Some things must get done regardless of what day or week it is.

I realized that I would have appreciated a more thorough understanding of my superior's expectations when I accepted the promotion. But I also knew it was on me to be accountable for the responsibilities I accepted in my career.

Thankfully, I didn't sacrifice everything in my personal life for NutriCorp. Just like summer eventually came to Minneapolis, things in my love life had been heating up. After being in Minnesota for a while and settled into his new job, John asked me to marry him. I thought, "Sure, I've known him for so long. What could possibly go wrong?"

CHAPTER 6

Pregnancy, Promotion, and a Vision from God

Shortly after getting married, John and I learned we were having a baby. We were both happy about the pregnancy, but I was literally on cloud nine! The first several months of my pregnancy progressed smoothly. I didn't have morning sickness.

During my pregnancy, I applied for a promotion. If I received it, we would need to move to Tennessee. We would both be closer to our families. After discussing the opportunity with John, he decided he would go back to school to get his master's degree if we wound up moving. Since I had his blessing, I applied for the position.

About three months later, though, I noticed my husband acting differently. I kept asking him what was wrong, but he would not tell me. In my gut, I knew there was a serious problem. I convinced myself I was the cause, so I scheduled an appointment with a therapist through my job's EAP (Employee Assistance Program). After a few sessions, the therapist recommended that John come in with me. At first, he didn't want to go, but he eventually agreed.

We had several sessions, and after some time John revealed the truth. My success intimidated him. He didn't think I needed him at all. I couldn't believe what I heard.

"I need you for what money can't buy: your love and companionship," I reassured him.

John seemed to hear me and tried to adapt. I tried to be hopeful. I often walked around on eggshells around him. I told myself that everything would be fine. Things improved somewhat, so I slowly let my guard down until things were back to normal between us.

About two-and-a-half months before our son was born, I found out I received the position in Tennessee. I ran home to tell my husband the good news. He said out of his mouth he was proud of me, but his body language didn't match. I asked him if he still wanted to move to Tennessee. He said yes, so we planned for the transition. The Master's program John applied to accepted him. He also located a personal trainer to work with him on his track skills. He had a dream of going to the Olympics, and I fully supported him. We decided to find a nanny that would take care of our son in our home.

Then, things totally changed. Although John always worked, one day, he accompanied me to one of my routine check-ups. That wasn’t something he ever did, but I welcomed his presence. During this visit, I learned that I had toxemia (a blood disorder). My doctor advised me to cease all activity to avoid raising my blood pressure to dangerous levels. He also said I needed to go to the hospital immediately. I begged the doctor to allow me to go home and pack my clothes and call my mother. I promised to meet him at the hospital afterward. I needed a moment to gather myself because the thought of what might happen next terrified me. The doctor agreed.

While we drove home from the doctor's office, John said, "You have not eaten, and it is past dinner time, so we need to get something to eat before going to the hospital." I agreed. I got home and called my mother. I told her she had to hurry and get there because I really needed her with me. She said she would be on the first available flight out. Since it was evening, she wouldn't arrive until 11 o'clock the next morning.

When I got off the phone, John yelled at me,

"You don't need your mother to come and take care of you. That is my job!"

I looked at him like he lost his mind. I explained that even though he was there, no one can ever take the place of my mother. He needed to get over it. Mama was coming to be with me. John picked a weird time to act like he was the man. He must have known my mother would go through the fire in hell to get to her child in need. He couldn't mean anything by it, I thought. So, I blew it off as nothing.

We went to a restaurant to eat. Our ride there was quiet. I was so nervous about going to the hospital, I didn't mind. I feared what was coming with my first child. While we were eating, John opened up. As he talked, I suspected he intercepted me at my appointment in order to arrange this dinner and have this conversation.

John shared that he always felt as though he competed with me. He didn't think I needed him or anyone; I could be successful without a spouse. I reminded John of what I said in therapy. I loved him and needed a partner for all the things that money can't buy and that a job title can't give. I told him I wanted to share life's experiences with him and live as one.

John replied, "I hear you, but you have your job and are doing well. I have a job too, but I also need to move forward. I am not going with you. You go on to Tennessee, and I will stay here and work. We can visit each other maybe once or twice a month."

I could not believe John was telling me this. I said,

"John, I did not get married to raise a child alone. We need to do this together. I don't need you to 'visit.' Our child needs a father who will be consistently present."

"Wow!" I thought to myself. "Am I really in this situation right now? I am worried about my child, worried about my marriage, and worried about how the rest of my life will turn out as I am on my way to the hospital."

Once we got the hospital and I settled into my room, a nurse prepared to give me an injection. I looked at my husband with tears rolling down my face and called his name. He said, "Yes?" but didn't move. The nurse looked at me and then looked at him. She said to John,

"She just needs you next to her."

I looked back at John. I asked him, "Are you going to stay with me tonight? They can bring in a roller bed for you." John looked at me dead in my eyes and said, "No, I have to go to work!" He then said he wasn't picking my mother up from the airport.

I told him, "Ok. No problem." Then he left the room. Hurt and anger boiled inside me. John was walking out on me and his child. I turned over in the bed in disbelief. I gathered myself together enough to use the hospital phone to call my girlfriend. I asked her to pick up my mother in the morning, and she agreed.

I had never been so glad to see Mama than when she arrived in my hospital room the next morning! She sat with me as I told her everything that happened with John. Mama excused herself to go to the chapel. She said she needed God before she became the devil! I knew what that meant; she was furious with John. Mama stayed with me in the hospital for the next two days. I hated every minute I was there. When my doctor came in to see me, I had a meltdown.

"Please, please let me go home," I begged. "My mother is here to help me, and I would do whatever I needed to do so I can go home." He agreed to let me go under the condition of strict bedrest until I was ready to deliver the baby.

At home, I could only get out of bed to use the bathroom. I refrained from doing even simple tasks such as brushing my hair for fear it would raise my blood pressure. Everything was fine until John decided he wanted to have sex with me. I looked at him in disbelief. All of our problems aside, I explained that I couldn't have sex because it would increase my blood pressure for sure and possibly harm our baby.

John didn't care. He thought he owned my body and expected me to respond to him when he demanded. He tried to force himself on me, and I screamed. Mama came running into the room. She gave him a piece of her mind and then tried pushing him down the steps. Mama told John he needed to leave the house.

My mind and heart were racing. I kept asking myself, "Did my husband just try to rape me? How can that be possible?" I tried to rationalize it. That couldn't be an attempt at rape because he was my husband. But I knew better.

Two weeks later, I was 32 weeks pregnant. When I met with my Obstetrician for my checkup, the doctor said it was time to deliver the baby via c-section. I admitted myself to the hospital. As they were checking to see if my baby's lungs were healthy enough for delivery, the needle broke in my stomach. The medical team was able to remove the needle and perform another test. Thankfully, the baby's lungs were mature enough.

The hospital's administrative staff gave me documents to sign to proceed with my c-section. I expressed my wishes: if they ever needed to choose between my life or my son's, I wanted my baby saved. Mama didn't like my decision, but she respected my wishes. Instead of arguing with me, she made another trip to the chapel.

As they prepared me for surgery, my mother convinced me to call my husband and let him know our child was about to be born. I didn't want to make that call, but I knew Mama was right. I called, and John came to the hospital. Mama and John were in the delivery room as Arthur was born.

But even though the delivery progressed smoothly, I wasn't ok. Shortly after childbirth, my vitals dropped. Ultimately, my heartbeat stopped. While the medical team tried to resuscitate me, the sounds of life drifted away. I lost consciousness for several minutes.

I had a vision. I saw what looked like the outside of Heaven. I saw Jesus on a horse that was standing next to large, pearl white gates. I was on my knees with my hands held out to Him. I asked,

"Can I please come in?"

Jesus responded and said, "No, it is not your time. I want you to go back and give opportunities to those who have been discounted. You help them succeed."

I was a little disappointed, and yet at peace. It was the most beautiful experience I've ever had. Then I slowly felt myself wake up. When I opened my eyes, I saw my mother crying over me. I consoled her.

"Mama," I said. "Why are you crying? I just saw Jesus. He said is not my time yet. God revealed my purpose." I had such a feeling of peace. I knew no matter what happened, I would be just fine!

Arthur was born at just four pounds three ounces but dropped to three pounds 11 ounces after birth. He had to stay in the hospital to gain weight. I spent the next three weeks traveling back and forth to the hospital to feed him because my baby wouldn't eat for anyone but me. It was November. There was over three feet of snow on the ground, and it was freezing. It was hard on me, but nothing would keep me away from my son. At the end of the third week, I begged the doctor to let me take him home, and I promised I would get him to five pounds. My negotiation skills worked, and I took Arthur home. He was up to five pounds after just seven days at home with his mommy. As I said, I knew everything would be fine.

CHAPTER 7

Diary of a Successful Black Single Mother

In the winter of 1988, I prepared for my big promotion and move to Tennessee. I was happy about my professional accomplishments, but on a personal level, I felt empty. Arthur and I weren't enough of a reason for John to come along. John told me I wasn't the problem. He wanted someone who needed him financially. At the company where we worked, many of his female colleagues were on government assistance. They were all desperate for a man to take care of them and their children financially. As he talked more about his work environment and what he wanted, I knew our marriage was over. At that point, I shifted my mindset. I vowed to myself to do whatever it takes to continue progressing in my career and to be a great mother.

The more I reflected on our situation, the more baffled I became. How did I get here? I had known John for fifteen years; wasn't that long enough to have a successful relationship? They always said you should marry your friend because it is a crucial component in the foundation of romantic relationships. Well, that is what I did. So why was I about to get a divorce?

The lesson I learned is that not every male friend should be a husband even if you love them. True, you want your husband to be a friend, but it takes more than that to make a marriage last. I had to realize that when a man is intimidated by your success and not a genuine supporter, the relationship won't work. It is also imperative you support their dreams. Relationships are two-way streets. Even though my marriage was over, I knew my life wasn't over. God has given me a second chance at life, and I had a purpose to fulfill. I was not giving up on my hopes and dreams.

Moving to Tennessee was scary. I was alone with a baby. I didn't know anyone there. I had to figure life out quickly. First, I had to situate my son. I didn't want him going to daycare since he was premature. I needed his immune system to build up and didn't want him picking up other kid's germs. So, I was in search of a nanny. Google and Angie's List were not around yet, so I started with who I knew. My company was great and gave me the names of other employees who were using nannies.

I compiled a list of potential nannies. I interviewed them like the world was ending! I could not be too careful. I had to trust the person I selected completely. After the background reference checks came back positive, I hired someone. I asked her to begin work two weeks before I returned to working full-time. I had to make sure she knew how to care for my son.

Things seemed to work out well, so I felt comfortable getting back into career mode. My office wasn't too far from home, so I often dropped in during the day for surprise visits. I wanted to see my son, but I also wanted to check up on her. She never knew when to expect me. One day I came home, and things were just not right. Arthur was wet and crying while she sat on the phone, chatting away as if she had nothing to do. That pissed me off. I let her know I no longer needed her services. I asked her to get her things and leave. I paid her for that day and escorted her to the front door.

I sat down with my son and balled my eyes out. What was I going to do now? I gave myself a few more minutes to complete my pity party; then I sprang into action. I called my job and told them I wasn't feeling well and couldn't come back to the office that day. On the one hand, I felt a little guilty for telling a "white" lie. On the other hand, it wasn't a total lie. I told myself, "Your stomach is upset and tied up in knots!"

I needed a solution to my childcare dilemma immediately. I got on my knees and prayed. After I prayed, I called a friend of mine. I told her what happened. Thankfully, she knew someone that could be a good fit for me. By 8:30 pm, I had a new nanny. She came over at 8:45 pm that night so I could show her around. She interacted with my son for an hour before he went to bed. Arthur seemed to take to her so that was a real blessing.

Although, juggling life as a single parent and executive was often challenging, I enjoyed working for NutriCorp. My time there gave me a lot of tools for my professional toolbox. Each of my experiences taught me lessons that carried me forward both personally and professionally. One of the critical foundations I gained was learning the connection between business and Information Technology (IT). I learned the importance of technology being an enabler for company needs and not just something that was creative and looked cool. IT departments should never create solutions just for the sake of existence. Every piece of technology must serve a business need. It is critical to understand the business before you build anything in technology. I will be forever grateful for this opportunity as it truly set the foundation for the rest of my career.

After spending 19 months in Tennessee, I received an opportunity to work with another company, ChemSolve Tech. It required that I move to a small town: Jacksonville, Illinois. My first thoughts were, "Do I really want to live in a small town? I am young, and I want more to do for myself and my child. Is this sacrifice worth it?"

Two things helped sway my decision. First, the company would help me buy my first house. I could give my son a real home with space to play and grow up. I could not believe those kinds of perks existed at a manager level; I thought only executives received them. But their offer was legitimate.

Second, Jacksonville was only ninety minutes away from my family in St. Louis. That drive would be a breeze. When I lived in Tennessee, it was a five-hour drive. It was a great job opportunity. I was moving up the corporate ladder and getting great benefits. Small town aside, the opportunity seemed made for me. I was confident I could make it work. I felt like I won the lottery,

So, in the Fall of 1989, Arthur and I left Tennessee. My role at ChemSolve Tech was Director for Software Development and Operations. My responsibilities included the day-to-day operations and software development for two plants. I had staff members at both locations and worked on multiple IT projects.

On the one hand, I loved my job and my beautiful home. I felt like I was in heaven with my son. But on the other hand, I didn't like being alone. My emotions sometimes got the best of me. My now ex-husband told me that no one would ever want me. Similar to the negative words my professor told me, I replayed John's words in my head often. At times I believed them. When these moments occurred, I focused more on my son and spending time with him. Arthur was always the bright spot in my days. I knew he depended on me.

During the late 1980s and early 90s, there was a lot of talk in the media about black single mothers. No one thought we had what it takes to raise a child alone, and they certainly didn't see us having successful careers at the same time. These words made me work even harder. Since I lived closer to home now, I made sure Arthur spent plenty of quality time with his Uncle Tommy and with his Grandpa. I may not be a man, but that didn't mean I could not give him what he needed and have other men teach him the things that I couldn't. 'Tell me I can't, and I will show you I can,' became my mantra.

Sometimes, though, single motherhood and my career collided. One day I received a call from my son's daycare around 11:30 in the morning. He was sick. I had to pick him up immediately. The timing couldn't have been worse. Our company was in the middle of preparing for a major product launch. I flashed back to my earlier experience at NutriCorp and my vacation request. I knew I had a responsibility to my job, but I had an even more significant responsibility to my child. There were plenty of people on my team who could carry on in my absence of a few hours. I was the only one my son had. So, I sprang into action.

I called one of my girlfriends who was also a single parent; we helped each other often. I explained my situation and asked her if I could drop Arthur to her after I took him to the doctor's office. She agreed. I called the pediatrician and secured an appointment right away. My next step was to inform my boss. I walked into his office to let him that my son was sick, and I needed to pick him up immediately. I let him know I needed to be out of the office for just a few hours but would be back. His response took me back.

"You are responsible for this launch!" he said in frustration. "I did not hire you to have to take off to deal with your children. I hired you to do a job. So, do it!"

I looked at him like he had lost his mind. So many thoughts flowed through my head at that moment. But I knew I couldn't say what was really on my mind. I took a breath, adjusted my game face and responded.

"I take full responsibility for this launch," I said. "I will get done. I have always over delivered, and I won't stop now. But I must take care of my son. Do what you need to do, but I will be back!"

I walked out of his office. Lord knows, as I walked out of the main door, I was so nervous. I wondered if I would still have a job in a few hours. What would I do if my access badge didn't work? I couldn't dwell on 'what if.' As I drove towards the daycare, I said to myself, "My child comes first. God will take care of this situation."

As I approached the door to my office a few hours later, I said a silent prayer, hoping my badge still worked. Well, it did! To get to my office, I had to pass my boss's door. It took every bone in my body not to stop in and tell him off. I wanted to say,

"You have a wife at home to deal with your children. I have no one. My son depends on me, and I will be there to take care of his needs."

I had to settle for role-playing the situation in my head. I couldn't let my frustration show. Everyone knew I was a single parent and that I never slacked on my job. I had a playpen in my office and had brought my son in many times to play and sleep as I worked. I did everything for this company. Why was I dealing with this kind of situation? What company would allow this to occur?

I contemplated going to HR. I wondered if it would help. The company was predominately white males, and I was the only person of any color in management. I felt like all these men have wives at home or someone to care for their children. They will never understand my situation. The person in charge of HR was a white female. I took my chances with her thinking maybe she would understand.

I saw her in the break area and asked if I could speak to her. She told me, sure. I went to her office. I was scared out of my mind because I really didn't know how she would respond. I knew she was single and did not have children. I wondered if she could empathize with my situation. I took a deep breath and told her what happened.

"I'm sorry this occurred," she started. "But your manager was right in his expectations of you. Vicki, you need to realize that this was a predominantly male industry. They don't understand your situation as a woman and never will."

Then she got personal. "That's why I chose not to get married or have children."

I was shocked. I couldn't believe someone would let a job define what was right for them. Why would someone do this, I wondered to myself?

The HR director's voice snapped me back to the moment.

"Ultimately, it is your life, and you do what you feel you need to. But as for your career, keep in mind it is all about the business and the bottom line. Although we have people issues that come up, the company will always look at how it affects their bottom line." I politely thanked her for her input.

I walked out of her office speechless. I knew she was correct. But I didn't want to let my career define what I wanted for my personal life. I had died and had received a second chance at life. I saw things differently now.

I ultimately realized my boss didn't know how to handle the stress of the launch. No one else on the team could do my exact job. He panicked because if I could not perform, it would reflect poorly on him. He was responsible for the projects' overall success.

Even though I understood, it still disappointed me that a manager would ever respond to an employee having a sick child that way. There is no way I can ever perform at my peak level if I had to worry about my child's health or safety. It took me several weeks to get over my frustration completely, but I kept the experience in mind. It showed me what kind of boss I never wanted to be. Even though business comes first, I think there is still room for compassion and understanding while still getting things done. In my case, I had left explicit instructions for my team to ensure that the project would move along in my absence. In the end, the launch went off without a hitch.

CHAPTER 8

Bad Things Happen to Good People

Shortly after the project launch, I faced some medical challenges. I needed to have exploratory surgery. I didn't think it was a big deal, so I didn't alert my family. A friend took me to the hospital for the procedure. The hospital staff brought me the standard liability waiver forms to complete. I assumed everything would be fine, so I signed them.

The exploratory surgery was an outpatient procedure. I assumed I would be out of the hospital by the afternoon, but I already arranged for my friend to pick up my son. I drifted off under the anesthesia.

When I opened my eyes, my brother and mother were standing over me. I blinked in confusion. I immediately asked questions like, "What are you guys doing here?" and "When am I going home?"

Mama looked at me like I lost my mind.

“You are not going home; you just had major surgery!" She brought me up to speed on what happened. When my "minor" procedure upgraded to "major" surgery, my friend called my family because she felt they should know. Mama scolded me for not telling her even if I thought it was a minor procedure. She reminded me I didn’t have to do this alone. Then Tommy gave me a piece of his mind! Let’s just say I never made that mistake again!

I was diagnosed with endometriosis. It is a condition where the tissue that should typically line the uterus grows on the outside. In my case, scar tissue fused my organs. They did the best they could to correct the situation, but I wouldn't be able to have any more children. Since then, I experienced pain in my abdomen region every day. But even with this constant reminder, I didn’t take the doctor's words to heart; I hoped that one day I would have more children.

I ended up staying in the hospital for three days. Then I took a medical leave from work that lasted six weeks. I worked from home four of those weeks. This ordeal taught me always to be aware of my health and not to leave the people who care for me most out of the loop.

Besides my health issue, my time in Jacksonville was as uneventful as I feared it would be; there was nothing to do in that small town.

Sure, I loved my job, but I only ever went to work then went home to be with my son. Even though my family was only 90 minutes away, I still felt alone on a day-to-day basis. Occasionally I would take Arthur and drive to my parents for the weekend, but it was too much to do all the time. I never even thought about dating because I didn't believe there was anyone in that small town who would be remotely interested in me. Thankfully, I was wrong!

One day, a lovely gentleman (I'll call him Adam) asked me out. We met through a friend at work. When he asked, my mind fluttered with a million thoughts. First, I needed to figure out childcare. Then I was curious about where we would go because there wasn't much to do in the sleepy town. I reluctantly accepted his invitation and opted to meet him at the restaurant.

To my surprise, we had a great time! I enjoyed our conversation and his company. Adam was an engineer which I loved since I was in IT; we had much to talk about with each other. Adam seemed supportive of my career; he always asked me how things were going. I could not believe I met a man unintimidated by my success. It was a breath of fresh air.

Although we were never officially a couple, we continued to date casually throughout the rest of my time in Jacksonville. I think we both were looking for companionship and a way to spice up our lives. Our friendship made living there tolerable.

As I reached the two-year mark in Jacksonville, I got a call regarding another opportunity. The offer had many things going for it. First off, it would promote me into a higher position. Second, I would get to move to St. Louis… home sweet home! It seemed like an easy decision. But there was one hiccup. I needed to sell my home, so I could move. Well, that proved to be a non-issue too. The company bought my house from me; then they had a real estate agent handle offloading the asset. It allowed me to have the money for the down payment on my next home. I loved the perks and benefits that came with being an executive.

Arthur and I said goodbye to ChemSolv Tech and hello to MediSolve Global in 1991. I was so excited to be back in the same city as my parents and two of my siblings; this was a dream come true. I moved into a new home and began a great new job as the Director of Operations. In this new role, I started a brand-new global operations department. I noticed I had a trend in my career; I always received job offers and opportunities to create something new. Also, I was often the only minority or woman at the leadership level in Information Technology.

I must admit it was exciting and scary at the same time. In this role, both employees and contractors comprised my team. It was a new dynamic for me. Previously, my team members were all employees. I quickly learned that employees received priority and more benefits than contractors. I had a tough time swallowing this concept. I looked at each team member equally and did my best to treat everyone with the same amount of respect. We were all here to do a job and do it well. However, the policies of what I could do as a leader were different.

Initially, I did not understand why I couldn't use team member talents equally. IRS regulations make strict distinctions between employees and contractors and the benefits that the company receives accordingly. There is a reason companies sometimes prefer contractors over employees. The company doesn't have to worry about salary, taxes, and benefits with independent contractors. The contractor merely received a monthly retainer for their services.

One of the first challenges I had to deal with at MediSolve Global was a critical employee performance issue. The company is in the pharmaceutical industry. We partnered with hospitals and doctors to provide medications. We could not make mistakes when mixing the medication ingredients. If poorly manufactured pills ever got into the hands of customers, things could go bad quickly. Part of my responsibility was to ensure my team consistently followed protocol. Any mistakes could cause patient death. It would also have a negative impact on the company's brand, revenue, and legal bills.

One employee (I'll call him Bill) worked third shift. Bill managed the nightly tasks on the mainframe. These jobs showed the mixture and amount of chemicals for the drugs on the production run. He had worked for MediSolve Global for over 25 years. He was an older white man who wasn't happy about reporting to a young Black woman. He even told me he saw me as a "little girl" because of my age and lack of experiences.

I kept my professional game face on every day, so I could deal effectively with Bill. I consciously treated him with the same level of respect I showed all my other team members. I stuck to the rules and facts whenever I communicated with him.

One night I came into work unannounced. I wanted to see how things were going. I found Bill sleep on the job. Worse than that, he wreaked of alcohol. I woke him up and asked him what was wrong. He said nothing, but he was visibly drunk. I asked him the status of the job he was running. When I checked for myself, it failed while he slept.

At that moment, I knew this was a significant mistake. We couldn't sell this batch of products. Wasted raw materials was a massive loss for the company. Bill's actions were my responsibility. I stayed through the evening to get production back on track. I went home long enough to shower and return to work. My parents took Arthur to school for me.

That next morning, I informed both my boss and HR of what occurred. As expected, the costly mistake upset my boss. I told him I took full responsibility for my department, both good and bad and that I would deal with the situation. HR advised me to bring Bill in for a meeting and guide him into getting help through the EAP (Employee Assistance Program). The company's position was that we would support him in working through his issue but had to take time off from work until he could get a release.

Bill agreed. He went on a 60-day leave. During his absence, I couldn't hire a replacement or even a temp. The rest of the team had to pull together and support each other through heavier workloads during Bill's absence.

The day Bill returned, I welcomed him back warmly. I didn't mention his previous infraction. For two days, I shadowed him on his shift because protocols changed while he was out. On the third evening, I told him to have a good evening and to let me know if he needed anything.

Leaving the building that evening was one of the hardest things I ever did in my career. I had to trust Bill to do his job and do it well; I couldn't feasibly babysit him every night. The professionals declared Bill fit to return to work, so I needed to give him room to prove himself. But I was still nervous. He actions ultimately reflected on me. I also knew my boss was watching how I lead in this situation. I didn't want to fail, primarily on account of someone else. I don't know if I could survive another mess up.

I did not sleep well that evening. I came into the office the next day exhausted. To my delightful surprise, everything went well overnight. Bill did a great job. Bill continued to do a great job over the next two weeks. I was cautiously optimistic.

During the third week, I stopped into the office one evening for a different reason. While there, I checked in on Bill. I couldn't believe my eyes when I found him asleep again. I could tell he had been asleep for at least three hours because all the jobs which ran within that timeframe failed.

Here was another mess I needed to clean up. I had followed protocol, and I worked with Bill to the best of my ability. But, now I couldn't anymore. He either needed to go to another department or get a different job. I couldn't trust him as a member of my team.

I dreaded telling my boss what happened. Not surprisingly, he was furious! He let some "colorful" language fly, even though he knew it wasn't directly my fault. We lost a lot of money that night. The loss was so bad I had to go to the President's office and explain what occurred. I didn't shy away from my responsibility, but I told him the entire story and all the steps I previously took to work with Bill and correct the problem.

The President understood and appreciated me taking ownership over the problem. Then he asked me what I planned to do next. I looked the President straight in his eyes and said, "I will work with HR to get him removed one way or another: either to another department or out the door."

"I like out of the door!" the President replied.

The entire executive team was very supportive of my course of action. The execs told me it took courage to be that type of leader. They told me not to worry about the money; they knew somehow, I would make it up. Not long after, I recouped the losses Bill caused via another significant project that my superiors had given me. I was just thankful that the Executives understood. I truly know what it means to take the good, bad, and ugly as a leader for your team.

HR agreed with my determination, and we began the process of having Bill removed. To carry out the termination process, I had to come in during his shift and fire him. The guards would be with me and would escort him out of the building.

Even though it was the right course of action and the leadership team fully supported me, I didn't look forward to letting Bill go. MediSolve Global was his life; he had been there for nearly three decades. I didn't want to be the one to cut off his livelihood. But I also couldn't afford to be responsible for thousands of dollars' worth of losses or potential accidental death. I knew he wouldn't take kindly to being fired by this "little Black girl," but I had to do it. The next evening, I officially fired Bill.

Shock rippled through the team. When Bill was preparing to leave, I noticed a female contractor present who worked the shift with him. I'll call her Shelly. I later found out from some other teammates that Bill and Shelly were dating. I had no idea. I was so engrossed in work and in taking care of the team that I was clueless about their personal lives outside the office. After learning this information, I did not respond or say anything because I didn't think it was any of my business. Unfortunately, it soon became my business.

About a week after Bill's firing, I received a death threat on my voice mail at work and home. It was the first of many. For weeks, I continued receiving menacing messages. The person electronically disguised their voice. The person would curse violently and say things like, "Your turn is coming!" When it first happened, I thought someone was playing a sick joke on me. But when the menacing messages persisted, I got scared. Getting messages at work was one thing, but how did they get my home phone number? I lived alone with my son, and Arthur's safety was my primary concern.

I told my boss, HR, security, and anyone else at MediSolve Global I thought needed to know or could help me. They put a wiretap on my home phone. I felt like my privacy was being violated even though I gave them my permission. It was all so crazy! I couldn't figure out why I was going through that situation. After the tap had been on the phone for about 45 days, they still did not find the person because they didn't stay on the line long enough.

One night I drove home after picking up Arthur. A message was waiting for me on my garage door: "Nigger your ass is mine!"

Seriously? Was this 1955? No, it was 1991! I called the police and my parents. My parents wanted me to stay with them.

"No way!" I said. "No one will run me out of my house. That is what they expect me to do. I'll let Arthur go with you, but I'm staying in my house."

That argument didn't fly with Daddy. He put his foot down, so both Arthur and I stayed with them for the night. But not before I cleaned off the hateful message.

I went to work the next day with my game face intact and refused to appear shaken. But this day, my tormenter got sloppy. They left me another voicemail and elaborated on the message they left on my garage. The message was long enough to trace the call. And guess who the perpetrator was? Shelly! Apparently, without Bill there, her extra money stopped. But instead of dealing with Bill, she took her frustrations out on me. Now, she had more significant problems to deal with than a lack of income.

That is an ordeal I will never forget. I honestly felt bad for whatever challenges Bill faced that caused him to be an alcoholic. But as I had learned earlier in my career, our personal lives can't impede the responsibilities we commit to on our jobs. I struggled with my thoughts over how much of my team members' lives I should know. I preferred to keep my personal life separate and felt my team also had the right to their privacy. But if they were mixing business and pleasure, then it became my business. There were lots of conversations and debates about this at work.

Ultimately, as I moved forward in my career, I tried to be more observant of my team members. I wanted to make sure I understood as best I could any potential issues that could arise and affect their performance. Bad things can sometimes happen to good people, and you never know how someone will respond when their livelihood is threatened.

CHAPTER 9

Back to Love, Back to School

Speaking of personal lives, I met someone during my second year at MediSolve Global. I'll call him Ken. It was 1992, and I decided to open up to dating again. But I was very protective of Arthur. I had no intention of letting any man around my child unless I thought the relationship would be long-term.

Things with Ken seemed like they would work out. He had a good job based out of Texas. He traveled to St. Louis a lot, so we saw each other frequently enough. He had two children of his own and was adamant about not wanting anymore. Since my doctors told me I couldn't have any more children, I thought this might be a good match.

But secretly I still wanted to have another child. In fact, every night Arthur would pray for a little brother or sister. I never discouraged him. I said to him, "Who knows, it just might happen one day!" But I didn't share our hopes with Ken. After dating for almost three years, we began the engagement conversation.

The situation with Bill and Shelly aside, my career at MediSolve Global progressed nicely. I received a promotion to Director of IT Operations and International Customer Support. Part of my role included launching and managing a new group. With an expanded team came more responsibilities, but I thrived on the challenge.

Firing Bill was probably my least favorite experience in my career up to that point. Unfortunately, I was about to have more experiences like it. Market conditions changed, and the business needed to adjust. The top executives initiated two rounds of layoffs at separate times which affected 250 people. Due to the sensitive information we managed, every time they fired someone, security escorted the person first to their desk to gather their belongings, then to the door.

As the Director of IT, I took part in the process. They notified me when the employee entered the conference room for their discussion. During the brief meeting, I disconnected their email. As a deterrent to behaviors getting out of control, they stationed undercover police officers in the lobby and parking lots.

No matter how many times it happened, being a part of the termination process never got any easier for me. They were good people losing their livelihoods. They did nothing wrong neither violated any policies. But no matter how much I empathized with their situation, I needed to keep my professional game face on and just do my job. I understood that markets changed, and the business needed to adjust, but I hated how those business decisions affected people so personally.

I must admit this was a hard lesson to learn, but it has helped me throughout my career. I learned the industry, market changes, and business models for the respective companies I worked for. I learned to consider all areas of business strategy and the companies' financial models, plus the personnel needs that keep the operation functioning. To remain competitive, customers, employees, and shareholders should expect changes will always be necessary at some point.

After the first set of layoffs, the CIO (Chief Information Officer) restructured the IT department. He chose to re-align functional areas to improve processes and meet the company's needs more efficiently. This reorganization directly impacted me. I reported directly to the CIO, and most of the functional areas of the IT organization reported to me. In the shuffle, I lost some of my staff. Some of my responsibilities shifted to other direct reports.

I took the change pretty hard. At first, I thought, "I worked so hard, and our team functioned well together. Why are you breaking us up after we were so successful?" In my mind, I knew it wasn't personal, but it felt like it was. The genuine relationships I built with my team members were fantastic. I felt like I was like letting my babies go. Honestly, I wanted to pop a big attitude. Instead, I hid my feelings behind my game face, walk into the office as if it didn't bother me, and kept doing my personal best.

About a week after the significant changes, I reflected on everything that happened as I drove to work. I realized I was blessed and should not complain about a thing. I could have been laid off along with everyone else. But I still had a job. I decided right then I would figure out a way to make this change work for me. Then I got a brilliant idea.

Rather than sulk, I would put another tool in my kit that would benefit me for the rest of my life. Since I had a lighter workload, I took advantage of one of my employee benefits and started taking classes towards my MBA. If I maintained a B average, the company paid my tuition. After graduation, I would get back all my book expenses as a gift.

I started my master's program in the fall of 1992 and completed it in 1994. It was probably the most challenging two years of my life. I juggled being a single parent with a full-time job and an intense class and personal study routine. I am amazed I found time to fit dating Ken in the mix, but I managed. Our relationship deepened. He supported me throughout my program and ultimately attended my graduation. After that, we talked about getting married.

But I didn't let my relationship with Ken or anything else take me off course. I had the motivation and determination not only to finish and earn that bonus check, but I wanted to finish in record time. I was equally determined not to allow my schedule to affect my ability to show my support to Arthur. I didn't miss being with him at basketball, baseball or karate. I wanted him to know I would always be there for him no matter what I was doing.

On Sundays, Arthur and I would sit at the kitchen table together. It was my study day, so he wanted to study too! He brought books to read or would color for hours while I worked. My other study time was during the week after he went to bed. My parents pitched in and helped with Arthur from time to time. It was a grueling schedule, but I would not have changed a thing.

During this whole time, I spent every single day in pain because of my endometriosis surgery a few years back. I could have ended the pain a while ago by having a hysterectomy. I decided against it because I always hoped to get pregnant again even though my chances were less than one half of 1%. My doctor also told me that whenever the pain got to be too much, come back to him and he would proceed with the surgery.

Well, early in 1995, the pain intensified. Working out was becoming challenging, and my abdomen area started to swell. I couldn't even close my jeans. So, I finally tapped out and went back to my doctor. I admitted that my pain had grown to be too much, so I wanted to proceed with the hysterectomy. The doctor ran a battery of routine tests on me to check me out before scheduling the surgery. He came back in the room and said,

"I know why your pain has intensified and why you can't put on your jeans. You are four months pregnant!"

At that moment I was floored, excited, and scared. I couldn't believe God had answered my prayers in such a spectacular way. My chances of getting pregnant were practically non-existent and here I was about to have my second baby! But I was nervous about telling Ken. He had been adamant about not having more children. I thought maybe the news might change his mind and he might get excited about this new development.

Much to my disappointment, Ken didn't change his mind. All talks of engagement and marriage ceased. I was already a single mother, and I had made sure Arthur lacked for nothing. Now it would just expand to include my new baby. Thankfully I had a lot of support from my family.

When my son Brandon was born in early November 1995, I did the right thing and called Ken to give him an opportunity to meet his son. Ken showed up towards the end of the month. My parents kept Arthur for me because I didn't know what would happen during this meeting and I didn't want my son to witness anything terrible. Brandon was overwhelmed when he met his father and cried the entire time, he held him. Ken handed Brandon back to me and said, "This really isn't what I want." He proceeded to pack his belongings and I drove him back to the airport. With me as his mama, Brandon would not lack for anything. Brandon, Arthur, and I would be just fine.

CHAPTER 10

Will My Real Husband Please Stand Up?

As the new year rolled in on January 1st, 1996, I was depressed. Here I was a highly successful, very educated Black woman with two beautiful boys that men didn't seem to want. My ex-husband's words about nobody wanted me because I was too strong and had a child rang in my ears. I must be in double jeopardy now that I had two children!

I felt as sad as I did in high school when my friends told me no one wanted to date, and Tommy had to come home from college to escort me to my Cotillion and prom. As I reflected on my string of failed relationships, I believed something was wrong with me. Perhaps I wasn't a woman that men wanted. I might never find a man or get married again.

The only thing I knew to do was to focus on what I could control. My career at MediSolve Global was going along well. During the time I was in school for my MBA, I received another promotion. I needed to continue to be successful to provide the best for my boys. I owned my home, and I was debt free aside from the mortgage and regular monthly bills. I knew I was a great mom to my sons. Plus, my family was nearby, and they were our support system. I simply had to keep my game face on and continue moving forward one step at a time.

Several months into 1996, my boss informed me of a new initiative he wanted me to spearhead. It required that we hire an outside consulting firm. As we went through the selection process, one of the "Big Five" firms were in the running. They sent an African American man to deliver the presentation. His name was Harold. He was good looking and very well dressed. Even though I noticed him, my depressed state wouldn't allow me to think much of him. Besides, this was business. I wasn't interested in crossing any boundaries.

Harold's firm ultimately won the bid and he became my point of contact. The project was on an accelerated pace, so Harold also spent a lot of time traveling to St. Louis to work with me directly. We were together frequently, but it was strictly business. Occasionally he was in town some weekends. I would have my parents babysit my sons, and Harold and I continued plugging away.

We had been working hard for most of the year. In November, I noticed a great concert that was coming into town in December. I thought it would be a great idea if I took a few members of the team out for a fun evening. I invited Harold to come along. He was often in St. Louis over the weekends and figured it might be a nice change of pace for him. I sent him an email floating the idea by him and he responded with, "Count me in."

When the week of the concert arrived a month later, a "perfect storm" of events prevented things from happening the way they should have. There was an emergency within my International Customer Service division. I needed to send a few of my team members out of town to handle the situation. It just so happened they were the same team members who also worked with me on the project with Harold. They wouldn't be available to come to the concert. That left only Harold and me to go together. I instantly got nervous. I didn't want it to seem like a date, neither did I want Harold to think I was trying to be sneaky.

I finally calmed my nerves down enough to send him an email explaining the situation. I let him know with only the two of us going he didn't have to attend if he didn't want to. I made sure I gave him an "out." He emailed me back, "I'm still in."

"Well, hot damn," I said. "Harold wants to go out with me!" I was giddy like a teenager. I instantly worried about what I would wear. Even though it wasn't officially a date, it wasn't exactly all business either. I didn't want to be too corporate or too enticing. On the day of the concert, a snowstorm rolled into town. By the time I arrived at his hotel to pick him up, I had received an alert about the show's cancellation. Oh, boy! I called Harold and gave him the bad news. He was not quite ready, yet so he invited me up to his room.

I waited for Harold in the seating area of his suite and asked him, "So what do you want to do now? We can go downstairs and have dinner and then I'll head home. But whatever you want to do is fine with me."

"Well, I don't want you to get stuck here if we have dinner. But you can at least have a drink with me." So that's what we did. I had stressed myself out for no reason! Nevertheless, Harold and I continued working together and soon the project was completed. Harold helped me make the final presentation. My boss and all my superiors were so pleased with the results. At the end of the engagement, there was a reception to celebrate the project. At that celebration, Harold asked me if I would go to dinner and a movie with him. I told him I would love to!

Harold and I continued dating. He traveled during the week for his job, but we always spent weekends together. Then in April 1997, he relocated to Atlanta, Georgia for his career. I went to help him move. I was excited about the change because it meant I could visit him in a city that was dear to my heart. I loved Atlanta. When I was a student at Spelman College, I would always say, "Atlanta will be my home one day."

Harold and I were very close and soon the day came when he asked me to marry him. My mind was reeling. "Did he really just say that to me? Am I dreaming? I can't be what he wants: not me!" But it was real.

Harold checked all of my boxes and accepted me the way I was. He was my biggest professional and personal supporter. With both of us in the IT field, my knowledge didn't intimidate him. He loved my independence and didn't care what anyone else thought. I was exactly what he wanted. I felt like I had won the lottery.

But me agreeing to marry him was one thing. I wanted us to talk to my oldest son Arthur who was nine years old at this time. We sat Arthur down, then Harold took a seat on the couch next to him. He told Arthur that he loved his mother and wanted to marry her. He asked Arthur what he thought. My son looked in Harold's eyes and said, "You really love my mom?"

Harold responded, "Yes." Arthur asked,

"Can I call you daddy?"

Harold said, "Sure!" Arthur responded,

"Then you can marry my mom!" That brought me to tears. I loved that Harold was not only a good match for me, but he was open to being a father to my sons. I couldn't help but think of the many nights I spent crying because I was alone and felt rejected. Just the previous January I worried that my ex-husband might be right, and I would not have someone special. My tears were joyful. I looked up and said within myself, "God, you really do know all things. You had this all planned for me. I simply needed to be patient and wait on You." Harold being in my life helped me deepen my faith in God because I had prayed and prayed and finally received my answer. I knew marrying Harold was the right decision.

Harold and I created a timeline and planned to be officially engaged in December 1997. Since I loved Atlanta so much, I knew I would be the one to relocate but I had to sell my house first. I figured the process might take several months, so I contracted a Real Estate agent to put my house on the market right away.

One weekend in July, I was visiting Harold in Atlanta, so we could start looking at houses together. It just so happened my Agent scheduled an open house for my property the same weekend. While Harold and I were house hunting, my agent called me on my cell phone. She said she had three offers on my house before the open house even began! She told me the highest offer and I instantly blurted out, "Take that offer!" Less than an hour later she called me back and said they accepted the offer, were in the process of signing the paperwork, and they wanted to take possession in 45 days.

I was excited about such a quick sale, but I was also nervous because I was about to be homeless in 45 days. I shared the news with Harold. He said, "I guess we better find a house this weekend because we will have to move you out pretty quickly!"

I went home to begin the preparations for leaving St. Louis and getting my sons enrolled in school in Atlanta as they would be getting started at the beginning of August. But I had to hit the pause button. I didn't want to make such a significant move to live with a man that wasn't my husband. I knew it was important to show my sons you must take responsibility for what you want. You have to treat a woman right and let your actions speak for themselves. One night as we were talking on the phone about our plans, I shared my concern with Harold.

"Look. I'm all for doing this," I said. "But I'm just not comfortable moving to Atlanta without being married. That's not the example I want to set for my sons."

"I respect that," Harold responded. "How about this? Call Vegas and find out how much it costs to get married."

So, I did. I got back to Harold with the information, and we decided to elope. The following weekend, I left the boys with their grandparents, but I didn't tell them what I was about to do. Harold flew into St. Louis that Friday night to pick me up and we flew to Las Vegas together. Saturday morning, I was walking by a slot machine and on a whim decided to play it. My 75 cents yielded me the jackpot! It happened to be the exact amount of money we were spending on our wedding package, hotel stay, and flights!

Our ceremony was taking place later in the afternoon in a beautiful, outdoor gazebo. We paid to have the ceremony recorded. We exchanged vows and kissed. Afterward, I asked to see the recording. The camera operator looked horrified.

"Oh, no!" he exclaimed.

"What's the matter?" I asked.

"The recording didn't take! You have to do it again. We can pick up from where you exchange vows."

"Oh, no the hell we won't!" I shot back. "We're going to start from the very beginning! We are eloping, and we need to have something to show our parents so let's do it again!"

After we exchanged vows twice and I reviewed the tape, I said to my husband, "I know we just got married twice, but you only get one free divorce and you better make it good!" Well, as of this publishing, it's been 21 years and counting, and he hasn't exercised that free divorce!

Back in St. Louis, reality struck. I was married! I had to leave my house in less than a month. I had to situate my sons in school in Atlanta. And I had to tell my boss that after six successful years at MediSolve Global, I would be leaving.

I had worked so hard to prove that I belonged and that I could handle responsibilities. I had earned my boss' trust the hard way. I knew I would have to do it again with a new boss somewhere else. I didn't let the thought discourage me. It was time for me to make a decision that prioritized my happiness over my career. I had been doing the reverse my entire adult life. My thought was jobs come and go, but the chance to create a real family is priceless. Families are here to stay.

I didn't think my boss would be pleased with my news, but I didn't anticipate his reaction. Boy, did he have a fit! He fussed and cussed. He even begged.

"You can't leave me!" he said. "You are the best employee I have ever had! I can trust you, and your work ethic is beyond impeccable. Can't you just commute back and forth?" His words were bittersweet. I was grateful for how much he valued me, but I felt like I was causing him harm. He really made me feel sad about leaving. As if that wasn't enough, the CEO had his words with me too. He did not want me to go either. Everyone was happy for me personally but were disappointed to be losing me.

I must say, that was the best any of my employers have ever made me feel. I had worked hard to prove myself over and over again. I put in the effort into learning about the business and move up. As a Black female executive in IT, I had earned the same respect my white male counterparts received. Simply put, it was a great experience in my professional journey.

CHAPTER 11

The Leader I Always Wanted to Have

It was August 1997. As I situated my boys and myself into our new life with Harold in Atlanta, I berated myself for having moved without a job.

"Are you crazy?" I constantly asked myself. "You left a damn good job and moved with no security!" My mind was playing tricks on me. I had to stop and tell myself, "Yes, I moved without having a new job secured. It was the right decision, and I will be ok!" After all I had been through and with my skill sets, nothing could hold me back. I was confident I would have a new job soon. Besides, I hadn't exactly been sitting around waiting for things to happen. The moment I knew I was moving, I applied for a variety of positions in Atlanta.

After two weeks in Atlanta, I got a phone call about one of those opportunities from a company I'll call NuGeniTech Software. I had a great introductory conversation and received an invitation to interview for the position. I determined to arm myself with as much information as possible. Of course, the internet wasn't what it is today, but that didn't stop me from getting my hands on as many press clippings and publicly available documentation as possible.

My nerves tried to get the better of me as my interview drew closer. I knew I had to pull it together. I had learned through other leadership classes that an interview is just a conversation about you. Who knows you better than yourself? No one. So, tell your story. Another strategy I reminded myself of was to ask questions that showed I had knowledge of the company's inner workings but want to learn more. So, I said to myself, "Game face, Vicki! You got this. Go and do your thing."

On the day of the interview, I woke up early and probably changed clothes five times. I wanted to look my absolute best. I wanted to make a great first impression. I opted to wear a black skirt suit. I wasn't sure how they would react to a dress, so I went with a time-tested conservative look. I was new to Atlanta, and even though NuGeniTech's office was only 10 minutes from my house, I didn't want to be late.

I left an hour early and arrived in 10 minutes. I waited in my car because I didn't want to seem too eager. At the standard 15 minutes prior, I entered their office.

I had a fantastic interview experience. I was "in love" with the person I met. He was warm, welcoming, and cared about facts. And he was African American. For me, it spoke volumes about the company already. As he escorted me around the office, I saw nothing but different faces in a variety of roles. If things continued to proceed well, I saw myself making a home there.

I meet with other management members based in the Atlanta office. The company's headquarters was in the United Kingdom, and I secretly hoped I would get to travel to meet with some of the higher-ups. Well, the answer was no. The person responsible for the area from corporate could make the decision. He came to Atlanta to meet with me.

In the end, they offered me the job. Once I started there, I learned that young man I liked so much in the interview process would be one of my direct reports. They had offered him my position but decided he didn't want it. So, he was hiring his boss. I was shocked because I didn't think people ever passed on a promotion.

In my executive role at NuGeniTech Software, the technical support team reported to me and partnered with the sales team. I managed the Atlanta Office. I also had the opportunity to build the customer relations team for the USA. The software development happened internationally so, in my role, I had the chance to travel and learn more about how the business functioned in different environments.

One thing I loved about NuGeniTech Software was that they followed "The Balance Scorecard" method, popularized by Robert S. Kaplan and David P. Norton in their book of the same name. The book and its principles became an excellent foundation for understanding a company's strategy. Everyone at NuGeniTech was reading the book and applying the concepts. I thought this was a remarkable global company, and I loved being there.

Shortly after moving to Atlanta, my husband had made it very clear that he wanted to adopt the boys legally. I cried tears of joy for days. Brandon didn't understand what was going on because he was only two years old, but Arthur was thrilled. To proceed, we needed to have one year of residency in the State of Georgia. When the year was up, we set things in motion and the court scheduled a date for us. This was the first time in life I couldn't wait to get to a courthouse to see a judge! My oldest son wanted his name changed. The judge granted his wish. Both my son's received new birth certificates with their new last names.

It was an awesome day for my family. I was happy on all fronts and was so in love with my husband. Marrying him was the right decision. My pattern of bad relationships was finally broken. I was excited because for the first time in my life, not only was my career thriving but so was my love life. Better still, I was in a relationship with someone who was elated to talk with me about what I did for a living. He always showed me he was as proud and supportive of me as I was of him. I honestly felt like the wealthiest woman in the world.

My departments at NuGeniTech were thriving and doing great work. I developed a rock-solid team. But a little over a year into my position, I felt the winds of change blowing. The business had been doing well, but then the US market performance declined. I was privy to some conversations as part of the leadership team, but not all. The only information shared with me was that they were going to start seeking ways to reduce expenses.

Well, this wasn't my first rodeo. I knew what "reduce expenses" meant. A company's largest expenditure is its investment in employee salaries and benefits. My experience with large-scale layoffs at MediSolve Global came flooding back into my head. No one ever said it to me, but my intuition told me that NuGeniTech would probably close the Atlanta office and move operations either to headquarters or another international office. As far as I was concerned, the handwriting on the wall as clear as day.

I knew I needed to start putting feelers out for a new job. I didn't know how fast or how slowly NuGeniTech would move on their initiatives to "reduce expenses." Then I thought about my current team. As I reflected on how horrible and helpless, I felt during MediSolve Globals' layoffs, I wondered if I could prepare my team to get ahead of the imminent storm that was coming without them knowing. Was there anything I could do to help them before they lost their livelihood?

I had a lot of great friends who worked in the placement business. One friend worked for a large placement firm. I'll call him Brian. He was continually looking for talent to fill the plethora of open positions he always seemed to have. Brian would periodically call me to go to lunch with him to find out if anyone in my network might be a fit for his opportunities. He happened to call me during this time frame, so I went to lunch with him.

As we were talking, I asked what types of roles he had available. After explaining, I provided him with the names of people on my team, without him knowing where they came from. He was very grateful for the leads. I felt conflicted. I wondered if I was doing the right thing? I felt disloyal to my responsibilities at NuGeniTech.

On the other hand, I knew what was about to happen, even if no one said anything. They were about to impact my team. I knew the right thing to do was to be as helpful to my team as I possibly could without alarming them or violating the company's code of ethics. They were great people and didn't deserve to be laid off without help, especially if I could help them.

I never told anyone I gave their names to a recruiter. But over the next two weeks, my team members quietly slipped into my office one by one. Their stories were the same. They had received calls about potential job opportunities and were feeling conflicted. They wanted to explore the possibilities, but they loved working for me and didn't want to leave. I gave them each the same speech.

Part of my responsibility to them as a leader was to make sure they had opportunities for growth. I told them they should never let their perceived loyalty to any individual or company stop them from a potential move forward. I encouraged them to take the interviews because it couldn't hurt to see where things might lead. If nothing happened, no harm, no foul. If someone made them an offer, then it would be decision time. They left my office relieved, and I continued to pray that I was doing the right thing.

Finally, the day I expected arrived. I got the call that I had to meet with the leaders. In that meeting, they informed me my team was being laid off. I was to let everyone go on a Tuesday and my final day would be Wednesday. It was easy for me to keep my game face on in that meeting because I already had another position lined up. Even better, almost all of my team members had either secured another role or was heavy in the interview process. I was so happy for them.

I questioned myself at the beginning, but now I felt vindicated. I concluded that as long as I did what I believed was right with no malicious intent behind it, I was ok. I did not violate any company policies. I did nothing illegal or unethical. I never broke leadership protocol to gossip or tell my team members my hunches. In the end, giving Brian my team members' names was the best way I could help them. They were such awesome people it was no surprise that other companies wanted to hire them.

From that point on in my career, I believed it was possible to keep your game face on and do your job while maintaining your humanity. I had figured out how to care for people in the process. Being a great leader meant allowing others to spread their wings. I didn't believe in holding someone back just because it was convenient for me. At the end of the day, it is all business, not only for the company but the employees too. I was happy that I could be the type of leader to my team that I always wanted to have. Even if they didn't know it, I was excited to be a blessing to them. I felt like I was living out a part of the purpose God had revealed in my vision ten years prior.

Before I left NuGeniTech, I had two more significant learning experiences. My direct boss was great, and I truly admired her. She had to struggle as a woman from the UK to prove herself continually to others. She was brilliant at software development and was an essential part of the brains of the operation.

Once my boss gave me my termination packet, she asked if I would come in the next day (at no pay) and help her pack up the office. I agreed, even though I could have said no. I knew they needed the help, and I did not want to burn a bridge. I wanted to show I was a team player to the end. You never know how a well-maintained professional connection can help you in the future.

Finally, I think the hardest thing for me was to learn that a severance package is a gift from the company; they don't have to offer one. The only thing a company is obligated to give departing employees is any accrued vacation. When companies do give you a severance package, they are being nice and are trying to be helpful to their former employees. None of us received a severance package. NuGeniTech only gave us our unused vacation pay. After all, they were laying us off because they were trying to reduce expenses. I was tempted to think my two successful years at the company deserved more but ultimately, I decided not to take it personally.

One week after my last day at NuGeniTech Software, I started a new position at National InfoMedia Network, a TV network and media company based in Atlanta. My role was Director, Solution Center. I would work closely with my new boss to create a new department that would provide support for all the company's products. I was excited to build something from scratch again. There were several business problems we needed to solve and a good deal of metrics to meet.

Part of my challenge from the outset was to convince internal departments to allow our new department to handle their support when they were accustomed to doing their own thing. Although I was prepared with a long list of benefits and could directly deal with concerns, I knew if I came on too strong, I wouldn't get 100% compliance. I knew the leaders of the various departments thought I was young. Not to mention, I was the only Black executive. I felt the pressure and knew all eyes were on me from the moment I walked in the door. I had to tread carefully to win everyone over. I could not blow my chance.

I spent my initial days and weeks at National InfoMedia Network visiting each department and shadowing the people who developed the products and conducted the services. I invested the time to learn them and their business. I learned what they considered essential, understood how they defined success, and which metrics they viewed as critical. After spending time in each department, I was in an excellent position to have conversations with the decision makers because now I could speak the language of what was important to each of them.

I set up individual meetings with the team leaders to share with them how my new department could help them reach their goals. I took care to show them how I could make their jobs easier. I showed them how our department would be adding value to their work. I am happy to say that every single department eagerly jumped on board and fully complied with the in-house support team. I was off to a great start.

During my first year at National InfoMedia Network, we had a problem with a piece of equipment on the roof. As a result, water leaked everywhere! Everyone showed up in an all-hands-on-deck fashion to help clean up. It was a real team effort where title didn't matter. It was great to see my boss, other executives, and my peers work so hard to take care of the issue. After that experience, I felt as though I were part of a great work family.

One of my responsibilities was vendor management. In that capacity, I had the pleasure of working with some great individuals from other companies. One of the women with whom I formed a great relationship with was the President of a non-profit organization called Women in Technology. Their mission was to support each other from a senior level perspective. There was a Board of Directors to help plan this program and move the organization forward. I was humbled and honored when she asked me to join them. I knew I would have another opportunity to learn from others.

Once again, I found myself as the only Black woman in the upper echelon of leadership. That wasn't a shock to me. But what I found unusual was the way the other board members opened their arms and accepted me. I grew accustomed to proving I had earned my seat at the table. Granted, I was always proving myself to men. So being a part of Women in Technology was a breath of fresh air. I had a voice and could express my thoughts on the topics we discussed. The subjects were leadership issues and technology challenges.

It was the beginning of a long relationship with a fantastic organization. I was able to take part in a group that has evolved over the past 18 years since I joined. We are now known as "THE" organization for women in STEAM (Science, Technology, Engineering, Arts and Math). We are instrumental in helping young ladies go from the classroom to the boardroom by giving them the information and tools to be adequately equipped to work in this industry. Ultimately, I became President of the Foundation Board and then President of WIT. I've also become a member of the Advisory Board.

I have been so grateful for the experience. I had learned early in my career that having a position on a Board of Director was an essential part of executive leadership. Leadership is not just about what you do on your job. It is also about contributing to the communities you influence. You need to establish your presence and personal brand. Being a part of this organization was a natural fit for me because I was passionate about my career and wanted to see more women excel in the industry the way I had.

CHAPTER 12

Adventures in Diversity

My time at National InfoMedia Network progressed well. I quickly earned a promotion to VP of Technical Operations and Customer Support. Within two years, I earned another promotion, this time to VP of Project Management, Technical Support and Customer Operations. Before I finally left in 2004, I briefly held a new position as the General Manager of Radio and Newspapers. But I am getting a little ahead of myself.

The early 2000s was an exciting time for me in my career. I had opportunities to grow, not only within the positions I held, but also outside my job. Getting involved with Women in Technology in 1999 was just the beginning of my involvement in various organizations and being involved in ushering in real change. While I had often been the only minority, or only woman, or only black person (sometimes I checked all three boxes) in management or executive leadership, I took part in initiatives which increased diversity at the companies I worked for and in my industry.

For example, I joined the National Association for Multi-ethnicity in Communications (NAMIC). Their mission is to advance multi-ethnic diversity in the communications industry. I immediately became an active member. I wanted to learn about other businesses in the field while expanding my network. I eventually got involved in leadership, holding many officer's roles. Ultimately, I became President of my chapter. I enjoyed the conferences the most. We regularly discussed how to improve diversity and how to improve the representation of women and minorities.

I took the message and mission to heart. I reflected on what I had been learning about diversity methodologies. Diversity wasn't just skin deep. Diversity of thought in an organization is just as important as having diversity in gender, race, age, and religious beliefs. Critical to a company's continued growth and relevance in the new millennium is having individuals with different perspectives at all levels of leadership. I started thinking specifically about National InfoMedia Network. I contemplated how to help our company stand out as a leader in diversity efforts. What would I need to do to get started? Who could help me solve this problem?

Eventually I came up with a brilliant way to introduce my ideas. The CEO of National InfoMedia Network loved to read. I wondered what he would do if I sent him a book by one of my favorite thought leaders in the diversity space? Not long after this idea popped into my head, I got a chance to test out my long shot.

One day, the CEO and I randomly entered an elevator at the same time. I took a calculated risk. After greeting him, I asked if I could have five minutes with him whenever he had the opportunity; it wasn't urgent. He said ok. To my surprise, he called me into his office the next day. Adrenalin coursed through my body as I made my way to see him. I tossed around different versions of what I wanted to say in my head and tried to anticipate his reaction to each. I wondered if I was about to step out of turn, but it was too late to back out. I had reached his office.

I took a deep breath, put on my game face, and said my peace. I opened by letting him know I was aware of his affinity for reading. I told him I had a book he might find interesting, then I handed it to him. If the book resonated with him, I wanted the opportunity to discuss an idea with him. He agreed.

I assumed I wouldn't hear anything for a few weeks, but to my surprise, he finished the book quickly and scheduled a time to meet with me. He said he found the book compelling and wanted to know my idea. I told him I thought National InfoMedia Network needed a standard diversity methodology with a common language to speak as an organization. We needed to have certified instructors inside the company and train everyone. It was a non-threatening way to start addressing diversity. He loved the idea and asked me to work with HR and professional development area to get this going. I had to provide a budget and a plan.

I was excited to have my CEO's support. I got to work right away. I met with the person over professional development to craft the training and all the logistics. We offered the first round of training to the executive team. They bought into the idea right away. They saw how this methodology could change the company's culture and help us meet our objectives.

Not long after the executive training, I attended an industry event where our CEO spoke. He talked about our diversity efforts with pride. He mentioned, "I have to give credit to an employee who recommended a book for me to read. My light bulbs went off all over the place and I was sold." I sat there knowing he meant me. At that moment, I mentally patted myself on the back for doing something out of my comfort zone. My boldness still surprised me; it was risky, and the results might have been different. But I was proud that I was helping to influence the company in such a significant manner.

Soon after the executive team's training, we developed a diversity council. I chaired the council and other minority leaders within the company joined me. I continued as a certified trainer and helped with issues across the company. Of course, this was beside my regular responsibilities. But I knew taking on different challenges was critical to my continued professional growth. The opportunities increased within the council. We had hosted events, seminars, had outside speakers come in, and more.

Our parent company loved our inventiveness and progress. This initiative gave some of our leaders a platform to discuss diversity at various industry events, which elevated their personal brand alongside the company's brand. Our peers viewed us as innovative and progressive. Every time we needed diverse talent to take part in activities, our selection was limited; we chose the same people repeatedly. We all knew this had to get better, and eventually, the company improved over time.

Not long afterward, I was hand-picked to take part in an invitation-only leadership development program within the company. The goal was to help us become self-aware and better leaders. Part of the process included our teams providing anonymous feedback on our leadership style. The feedback I received from my team was that they knew I had high expectations for them, but I was fair. I appreciated that because I was always conscious about balancing my team's needs with the needs of the company.

However, some other comments bothered me. My team perceived me as "working all the time." They believed they had to emulate my work habits to get ahead. I never really presumed people were watching me that closely, especially other minorities. They viewed me as a role model and wanted to experience the same success. The irony was I didn't "work all the time" to achieve success. I worked all the time because it was fun for me. It didn't feel like a grind or drudgery. I knew I needed to communicate to my team that they should work in a manner that would give them their best, high-quality results in a timely fashion. They shouldn't do things the same way I or anyone else did.

A new concept this training introduced me to was mentoring and grooming new leaders. The idea intrigued me, and I wondered what my superiors meant by it. What is mentoring and how does it work? How do we mentor others inside the company? Around the same time, I kept hearing about the concept of being a sponsor. I wondered what a sponsor was and how it compared to being a mentor.

What I've since learned is this: a mentor will help you work through your career challenges. It is possible to (and probably recommended that you) have multiple mentors. Your mentors do not all need to be of your same gender or ethnicity; having a diversity of perspectives can only benefit you.

Furthermore, you should be clear about what you would like to learn from each of your mentors. One mentor might help you with your professional attire and fitting into the company's culture. You might engage another mentor to learn about how they built effective teams. It is impossible for one mentor to teach you everything you need to know to be successful.

By contrast, a sponsor is a person who has a "voice" among the decision makers. They can be inside your company, or they could be part of other companies, groups, or professional associations. These people know you well and can speak to others about your talents and ability. The crazy thing is that sometimes, you may not know you have a sponsor. They might be a "fairy godmother" of sorts who has recognized your potential and advocates for your promotion, nominates you for a program, board membership, award, or another opportunity. Other times, your mentors can also serve as sponsors for you too. It is critical that you always do your best work because you are building your personal brand and reputation. You never know who is watching you. Cultivating relationships with people who could be mentors and sponsors for you is critical to your professional growth and indeed a gift!

Becoming a mentor and sponsor for others became a real passion for me from this point forward; it became part of my personal brand. I vowed to always be available for others, regardless of how busy I was. I would still "reach back with my rope and pull others up with me!" I had always done that, but now I was very intentional about it. Each week, I dedicated one hour to look for mentee "matches" and to help those I found. The process required that I be honest with them, so they could grow and develop. I would talk with them through the current challenges they were having on the job or help them in the process of getting their next opportunities.

As a part of my role on the Diversity Council at National InfoMedia Network, I helped to resolve any diversity issues which presented themselves. But there was one situation in particular which genuinely put all my training to the test. One day, a young man I'll call Mike came into my office to speak with me. He said he wanted to share something with me regarding diversity. I warmly invited him in.

Mike sat down. He told me personal details about his life. Mike had a wife and two children in high school. He confessed that although his life seemed ideal to others, he had not been happy for a long time. I asked if his dissatisfaction was personal or professional. He responded that his situation impacted both.

I grew worried. I couldn't figure out what Mike was trying to get off his chest. I wasn't a therapist, so I wondered if I was prepared to handle whatever he was about to tell me. Well, finally Mike confessed that he believed he was born the wrong gender. He tried fitting into everyone's definition of being a man, down to getting married, having children, and providing for his family. But he had reached a point where he could no longer deny that he identified as a female.

Mike shared with me he was planning to change his identity, including ultimately having gender reassignment surgery. Mike informed me that a part of his process was to start presenting himself as female. He planned to undergo therapy and several other steps before they would conduct the surgery. I said, ok. Then Mike took a deep breath and said what I believe was the point for his visit.

"On Monday morning, I will arrive to work as a woman, and I will have a different name."

"What is your new name?" I asked.

"You can call me Anne," Mike replied.

"Thanks for feeling comfortable enough to share something so personal with me," I replied. "What can I do to support you?"

Mike asked if I would tell the team and change his name tag. I assured him I would handle it.

When he walked out of my office, I was in shock! I didn't know what to think, but I knew I needed to be supportive of Mike's request. It was Friday afternoon. I needed to move quickly.

I called HR and shared the conversation. I said I could take care of the name tag, but we had to address the other teammates. They had a right to know, and we wanted Anne to be comfortable on Monday when she came to work.

HR and I called the team together to relay the information. In our briefing, we emphasized that we needed to respect Anne's choice as we would respect anyone else. It would not be acceptable to hear any comments regarding this issue. We had to commit to being professional. Most of the team members were open to the news. But a few had significant problems because they felt it went against their personal moral values. The biggest question people had was which bathroom she would use. Neither gender wanted Anne using their bathroom. I told them no problem; there was a handicap bathroom on the floor which she could use privately. We ended the meeting, and I put the name tag on her desk.

The real test came on Monday when Anne showed up to work. She was wearing a dress, pantyhose, makeup and nail polish. As Anne passed me in the hallway, I greeted her and said, "Good morning Anne." She replied, "Good morning," with a smile. She met her new name tag on her desk. She sat down to begin her day.

Part of Anne's work involved dealing with vendors. Several meetings were coming up. The first one was at 10:00 am. Anne was a part of that meeting. I knew I had to prepare the vendors for the change.

I called down to the receptionist and asked her to have our guests wait down there for me. I briefed them ahead of time so that there were no awkward moments. Thankfully, the meeting went smoothly. At the end of the day, Anne stopped by my office to thank me. She said she felt supported and still like a valuable part of the team. I was relieved to hear that.

Just as I had a responsibility to help Anne feel comfortable in her transition, I had a responsibility to help those who didn't feel comfortable with the situation. I had conversations with some people who had a hard time accepting someone else's desires that conflicted with their values. They wondered, "Don't I have the right to work at a company that didn't force me to compromise my morals?" My answer was, "Yes, you have the same right." Everyone has the right to work where you feel you are a "fit" for the culture. Every company's culture is different. If the environment is no longer a fit for you, then you may need to consider exploring your options. That might sound harsh, but the bottom line is that you have a job to do and teamwork is an integral part of getting your job done. It is what you are expected to do. So, whenever you find you can no longer work with your teammates in that environment, it may be time to change jobs.

About a year later, I was chosen to attend an all-women's industry leadership program. I was so excited because the acceptance process was selective. The experience was beneficial for both my personal development and my professional network. I built relationships with other women from different companies within the same industry. My participation in this organization helped me realized that each of us is a CEO. You are the CEO of "You, Inc." It helped me truly understand that I alone had accountability for my career; no one owed me anything. I had been focused on building a career since high school but now, I had a different level of understanding. I had to manage my behavior, my personal brand, my image, and the relationships that could propel me forward.

This group was a real haven for me. I felt free enough to let everything out in the open. We worked together to help each other. We discussed issues such as needing more women in the top ranks of companies. We mulled over what we can do to increase diversity in leadership roles. We examined possibilities on how we could help deepen male leadership's understanding of the importance of supporting diversity efforts. It was a true industry sister-hood.

My cohort bonded so powerfully that we stayed in touch and continued to support each other long after the program was over. These relationships were so strong I could pick up the phone and get advice on how to handle an issue or business problem and get help without being judged. Confidentiality was sacred in this group. In my world, this was hard to find. These kinds of relationships are priceless.

As I said earlier, the early 2000s was a fantastic time of growth for me. It was mostly due to the various groups and organizations I took part in. One such group was a global for-profit organization which invited me to chair their Board of Directors. I was honored to work with a leader who had the vision to expand technical knowledge around the world. I met Consulates from other countries and interface with entities outside the USA. I found the panel discussions and events powerful. I had a lot of fun and found serving on a board to be exciting. However, being a part of a board can cost you a lot of money.

Regardless, I would not have traded this assignment for anything. It gave me another level of understanding and exposure to business and diversity issues across the globe.

I learned so much from all my experiences to this point; I didn't think there was a business situation which could surprise me. But a unique incident occurred which changed that thought. It was 2004. By then, I had been at National InfoMedia Network for five years. I was discussing the performance review of one of my direct reports with the HR director before I delivered the results to her. She had performed above expectations and was great at her role and responsibilities. I wanted to promote her to Vice President. My title at the time was Senior Vice President. The HR director agreed she had done an excellent job, but he discouraged me from recommending the promotion.

"Oh no, don't promote her!" he said. "If you do, the execs might think they don't need you." His words shocked me. I couldn't believe he said that. I knew he was trying to look out for me, but I didn't feel comfortable holding someone back on my account. I knew the right thing was to promote her.

"Well, if that is the case," I responded, "Then I guess it is time for me to find another opportunity. She deserves this promotion!"

The young lady did receive her promotion, and they moved me into another role in the business. Shortly after this, I moved to another company.

CHAPTER 13

Actions Speak Louder Than Words

In 2004 a dream opportunity knocked on my door, and I had to answer. I always wanted to be a Chief Operating Officer. I couldn't pass up the chance. I said goodbye to my National InfoMedia Network family and said hello to the opportunity to work with a powerful, African American male CEO in the media industry at a company I'll call MediaAd Networks.

I took the role understanding there were several undesirable factors in play. For one, it was a lateral move financially. The company was smaller than any I previously worked for. Also, a private investment group owned the company. There was a strong possibility that the business might soon be sold. I didn't know how long I would have a job.

But the positives far outweighed the negatives for me. For one, for the first time, the CEO at a company I worked for looked like me.

He was a focused visionary, and I was excited to be under his leadership. Second, I would be a part of the Board and connect with different types of leaders. Third, I was getting my feet wet in a dream role.

I will never forget my first day. I had to travel out of town to meet the leaders. The CEO and VP of Operations met me at the hotel. The CEO introduced me to the VP; I'll call her Lisa. Lisa flipped her hair and gave me an icy 'Hi.' "Wow, what's her deal?" I wondered. Before long, I discovered the problem.

Lisa was a brilliant and talented young woman. As VP, she reported directly to the CEO. Lisa knew MediaAd Networks operations inside and out and was incredibly knowledgeable. But with me coming into the business as COO, she would have to report to me. To add insult to her injury, she had to train me. I was new to the industry and had a lot to learn. Lisa was my reluctant teacher. In her mind, she didn't see the need for my hiring. She certainly didn't appreciate having to report to an outsider. I immediately recognized that I had my work cut out for me trying to build a good working relationship with her.

It is important to note that the company had a strict culture from its previous CEO, and everyone followed policies 'by the book.' For example, if the rules required that you marked vacation time for a specific reason, that is what you did. No exceptions, no variations.

The new CEO wanted to improve the culture and get the most out of his excellent team. But culture changes require time and patience. I pondered how I would build a bridge with Lisa in this environment. I truly admired how bright she was and the strong relationships she had with the rest of the team. How was I going to help her understand that I wasn't against her, I was for her? I recognized that if I successfully won her over, it would go a long way with the other team members.

It was not an easy process. But my strategy was to let my actions speak louder than my words to show Lisa I was genuine and worthy of her trust. People will only accept change as their trust in you grows. I gave her praise when it was due and let her know I valued her input. Every time she did well, I also informed the CEO. I would always comment on her talents and strengths. If we had a problem, I only dealt with facts and asked lots of questions. I would ask for her thoughts and views on how to solve for the next time. I did not make it ok when we did not perform up to par.

I showed Lisa that I cared about her as a person. She was expecting her first child at the time. Throughout her pregnancy, she was always at work and continued to be a superstar. She forced herself to come to work and do her job because she didn't want to log too many sick or vacation days. She was saving them for when the baby was born.

Lisa was sitting in my office discussing a client. I could tell she wasn't doing well. I paused and asked her how she felt. She answered honestly.

"Lisa, go home and take care of yourself," I said. "You can work from there."

Her eyes got round like saucers in total shock.

"No, that's ok, I will stay," she responded. I told her she worked so damn hard, she had my permission to go home and work from there. I also told her it would not count against her sick time or anything else. Lisa reminded me of the rules and policy in the employee handbook.

"I have the authority to override that rule. Go home!" I insisted. Relief washed over her face. Lisa thanked me repeatedly.

"Well, I thank you for being a great team member on the team!"

The next day, I told her to stay home. She took part in meetings by phone and used the weekend to rest. That incident changed the tide in our relationship.

I loved being in my role at MediaAd Networks. Working with the investment group who owned the company gave me a different vantage point on business. It is very different when working for people who put their own money into a company and are expecting to see their returns. I learned hard but valuable lessons.

Some of the biggest lessons I learned came from temporary leading the sales team. The organization was undergoing leadership changes and I raised my hand to oversee that group in the interim. It was new for me, but I was confident I could make it work. There were weekly calls and financial targets to meet. I had fun going into the field with my team members to meet with customers. This was great as I could get to understand more of what the companies desired. But that is where my excitement ended.

I soon found out that leading a sales team is hard work. The leaders and the team members are always under pressure. We had a responsibility to make our projected numbers every single month. As the stress of the role took its toll on me, I questioned myself and wondered if I would fail. But I quickly turned my thoughts around. I asked myself, "How can you fail at your first attempt in learning something new?"

That is how I viewed the situation. I had learned a lot. I now knew I never wanted to manage a sales team again. I wouldn't mind if they were in my organization, but there would have to be a sales leader who dealt with the day-to-day issues. After dealing with the stress of hitting sales goals, clients who canceled meetings at the last minute, support issues and more, I had a newfound respect for salespeople and the leaders who managed them.

Even though it was very challenging, I wouldn't trade the experience for anything. I was grateful for the first-hand perspective I gained from being focused on the bottom line. It drove the point home for me that everything indeed is "just business" and not personal at all. Executives lead based on what will be best for the company and the ability to get a positive return. After all, don't each of us do this in our households? We do what we believe will benefit our family or ourselves based on the information available to us.

In December 2005, we sold the business, and I was out of a job. But I had an awesome time there. It's hard for me to put into words how much I learned in my short time. I added lessons to my career toolbox, and they definitely came in handy later on.

It seemed strange for me to enter 2006 without a job. I wanted to jump into a new position as soon as possible. But I had just been a

Chief Operating Officer. C-suite executive level jobs aren't a dime a dozen. I had to wait until a role became available that would fit my skill sets. I knew it would take time, but I was impatient.

I wanted a job offer immediately with a starting date a month away. Then I would take a little time to relax and then get back in the saddle. Time was passing, and I hadn't turned up a viable opportunity. I was getting restless and a little depressed. I wondered to myself, "I have excellent qualifications, and I am ready to go. Why isn't there a job for me?"

Not long after, I heard about an event through a friend of mine. Someone had invited me to a gathering of women, but I never saw the email. My girlfriend called me to ask if I was going because she had seen my name on the email distribution list. My response was they did not invite me. She quickly corrected me and told me I was on the list. Because I was not feeling positive about myself, I told her no. But my girlfriend didn't accept that. She said, "You are going even if I have to come and pick you up!" How could I argue with that?

All the way to the event, I worried about fitting in. I assumed everyone there would have a job and exciting things to talk about while I didn't. As negative thoughts continued flooding my mind, we stopped at an intersection. I looked at the red light and said to myself,

"Ok Vicki, no more thoughts like this. Game face on! You go in there with your smile and positive attitude. You can talk about how you just sold a company. That is an experience people don't have every day. Don't discredit your accomplishments just because you don't have a job at the moment."

After my pep talk, I felt better. We pulled up to the host's beautiful home, and I said to myself, "Let's do this!"

I found myself in the room with some fantastic women. I already knew many of them from participating in other groups, so we had a chance to catch up on each other's lives. When they talked about business and work, I stayed quiet and just listened. I will admit, the devil tried hard to get me back to that lousy thought process again, but I would not let him win. I had plans to go with my husband to his company's Christmas party that evening. That would be my cue to leave.

But instead, when I excused myself to call Harold, I didn't want to leave. I asked him,

"Do I have to go to your party? I am with some amazing women, and I am just now relaxing."

"Nope," he replied. "You don't have to come with me. Stay and enjoy yourself." So, I did. I ate good food, had a nice glass of wine and the evening kept improving. Then, something great happened. One woman in attendance was an executive at her company.

"Vicki, send me your resume," she said. "I might have an opportunity for you."

"Really?" I perked up.

"Yes," she replied. "You would be great at this role."

"No problem! As soon as I got home, you will have it!"

I was so glad my girlfriend convinced me to go. As I rode home, I hoped that the executive would be a woman of her word by putting my resume into the right hands.

"Lord," I prayed. "I hope this is the right job for me!"

I could not help getting excited. I tried to be optimistic but not overly anxious. That is hard to do when you are impatient and boy, was I impatient!

The interview process dragged on. I had phone interviews and in-person meetings. Then I got called back for more and more interviews.

"Gosh," I thought. "How many interviews do I need to have to get this job? Can't they see the position is already mine? Come on now!" I said to the decision makers in an imaginary conversation in my head. "Just make me an offer and let's move on with it!" Well, they must have heard me because they finally offered me the job. I was ecstatic about starting my new role.

Before starting my new job, I had reflected on one of the biggest lessons I had learned. You must get out and find out what is going on. It is fine to network, but relationships are critical. Networking is only as good as someone knowing your name and being willing to help you; it doesn't matter how well you know them. It was also great to know there are real sister supporters out there to help. Everyone is not in competition. The important thing is to have discernment and to understand the boundaries.

CHAPTER 14

Learning Different Leadership Styles

In April 2006, I started my new job. I'll call the company Nationwide Entertainment Corp. My title was Senior VP of Enterprise Performance and my role was to create a brand-new department within IT. They formed the position and team to help the company understand project investments and business impacts. I always got excited about building new departments. Not only did I get to develop a new team, but I got to establish and implement new operational methodologies for the company.

But first, I had to influence internal teams and leaders to change how they were operating. The only way for me to get them on board was to learn as much as possible about their groups. It reminded me of my time at National InfoMedia Network, so I deployed a similar strategy. Although sitting with each department increased my learning about how Nationwide Entertainment Corp functioned, not every business unit cared about my mission. They enjoyed their current autonomy and their own decisions as they saw fit.

I quickly realized that to them my presence was like "the corporate office trying to tell the field what to do and how to do it." In their minds, corporate had "no idea" what truly went on. I had my work cut out for me. I had to figure out what would give me the best success without setting off infighting and office politics.

I took the time to assess how many business leaders wanted the support and how many were entirely against it. In looking at this, I also observed and understood the relationships between leaders and how they interacted. I saw a variety of leadership styles. Through this process, I learned that most people characterized my boss (I'll call him Steve) as being difficult. I had never entered an environment where I received such passionate feedback about my boss before. I too was new, so I didn't want to prejudge my working relationship with Steve.

Even with all this information, I built my team, and we moved forward. I recruited Lisa, the VP from MediaAd Networks, to be my right hand. I trusted her, and we already had a great working rapport. It was one of the best decisions I ever made.

As I continued learning more about the various leaders of the organization, an incident occurred which I found revealing. I was about to have a meeting with Steve and several of the other executives. Small talk buzzed around the room before the meeting. The subject of Atlanta Public Schools came up. Various opinions floated around the table concerning the leadership of the school board and which side of town had "decent" education. Then, several of the executives discussed their children attending private schools.

I sat with my best game face on, just listening. Then one person in the room said,

"I would never send my child to public schools. They learn nothing and come out unprepared and dumb."

I was sure that my game face slipped, and everyone could see the frog jumping in my throat. I thought to myself,

"Wow is that how you all feel?" But I remained silent. The same person then asked everyone where their children attended school. I waited for him to reach me. When he asked, I said flatly,

"My kids go to public school. And, by the way, I graduated from a public school."

You could hear a pin drop. The person who called the meeting quickly said,

"Ok, let's get started!"

I stewed in my emotions as I endured the meeting. I was the only black person in the room, male or female, and there was one other woman. The rest were white men. They judged people before learning anything about them as individuals and it made me angry. Every public-school system is not the same. I took part in magnet programs and enrolled in college courses while still in high school. I leveraged it into a successful career. Clearly, not everyone who goes to public school comes out dumb!

I had to calm myself down. "Vicki," I told myself. "You must realize you are around privileged people. But not everyone who is financially well off has such a judgmental view of others." Then I challenged myself by wondering how I would use what I had just learned about those individuals to move forward and be successful.

Once the meeting concluded and we walked out of the room, no one said a word about the conversation. I reasoned that those in the room genuinely held those feelings otherwise they wouldn't have been comfortable saying what they did. I guess because everyone in the room was an executive or in upper management, they assumed everyone's kids were in private schools. I knew conversations like these happened, but never witnessed one. I found it interesting how they acted as though nothing happened when they put their foot in their mouths. I chalked it up to being another valuable lesson learned.

As an African American executive at this powerful, national corporation, I had a responsibility to be a mentor. I spent a lot of my time meeting with others throughout the company. It was my own "informal" mentorship program. I took part in formal ones as well, but the informal mentees proved to be much longer lasting relationships. Each one I mentored could tell I genuinely cared about them. But honestly, I've received more from them than they received from me. These relationships have been support systems for me too.

As my time at Nationwide Entertainment Corp progressed, I understood everyone's impressions of Steve. I thought he was a bright man with incredible ideas, but he was challenging to work with. I did my best not to let that bother me. Instead, I focused on how much I could learn from him in order to put more tools in my career toolkit.

One particular incident involving Steve stood out to me. Leadership asked me to speak on a panel one day. The purpose was to talk about our department's vision, goals, and our teams. These settings were always a double-edged sword. People asked questions that tested limits. They used humor or other means to get an answer to questions everyone had been whispering and wondering about behind leadership's back.

So, during this panel discussion, someone asked about our boss: "What is it like to work for Steve? Is he really that tough?" After reading the question from a card, the asker said,

"Ok, Vicki you answer the question. You will say anything!"

"Yes," I quickly responded. "As long as it is the truth!" I chose my next words carefully. "Steve has high expectations, and he likes to understand when things can't happen according to his thinking."

Although I kept my game face on, I didn't like being put on the spot. They wanted to see if my response would be "politically correct." I wasn't born yesterday. I wouldn't say anything that would harm me later. I was truthful, but the listener had to read between the lines. "Can't happen according to his thinking" could have easily been interpreted as things had to either go his way or no way.

I guess I didn't mess up in Steve's mind because shortly after this incident he promoted me. My new title was Senior VP of Digital Media and Enterprise performance. They asked me to lead another department, besides the one I had. Among others, I had a smart, brilliant and talented person reporting to me; I'll call her Erica. Erica knew her area inside and out and was extremely knowledgeable. She had an executive title and the authority to make things happen. So, I assumed this new assignment would be a piece of cake.

Well, not so much. Erica previously reported to Steve directly. Now, she reported to me. So, I had a bit of déjà vu; I had been down a similar path at National InfoMedia Network with Lisa.

Most of my challenges with Erica stemmed from having different leadership styles. I always conducted a weekly one-on-one meeting with everyone. It helped me stay abreast of what was happening. They could also discuss any issues or challenges in that forum. My one rule for my team was "no surprises." I didn't like getting blindsided. I always wanted to have an answer whenever my boss, another team leader, or a client called me.

Erica didn't provide a lot of information unless she thought it was absolutely necessary. Steve never required her to. Erica already had the authority to handle her situations, so she did. I respected that. But my peers still called me about problems even if they never called Erica.

I set my expectations with Erica, but on several occasions afterwards, I received phone calls about issues I knew nothing about. I spoke with Erica again. She told me I was a "micro-manager" and I wasn't allowing her to do her job. That was a hard pill to swallow as I thought I was only asking so I wouldn't be surprised. Was that asking too much?

Finding common ground with Erica was a challenge. She assumed I didn't trust her when, in fact, I respected and valued her opinions. Even though it was a tough journey, I didn't want to give up on having a good working relationship with Erica. I was conscious about showing her my support. We ended up having lots of conversations before we finally reached common ground. One thing Erica didn't realize at first was how often my peers in the business called me about problems before they called the person directly responsible. Once she understood my need for information wasn't an attack on her skills or abilities, she felt more comfortable sharing.

One of the biggest lessons I took away from my time at Nationwide Entertainment Corp was learning how to navigate different leadership styles. I had the time to form my own impression of working with Steve. As I mentioned before, he was smart and had great ideas. He was always thinking of a way to change things up or had a different approach for issues which arose within the organization. It meant his teams had to be highly adaptable and able to flow with his changes. It was problematic when trying to complete projects. Team members grew disgruntled when new parameters were added continuously, causing the project's finish line to slip further out of view. To increase the difficulty level, team members didn't always have enough resources to make it all work.

I was constantly asking myself, "How can I best help my team under these circumstances?" How do I handle working with difficult leaders? What do I do when my boss and I disagree about the direction I should steer my team in? Those questions were never easy to resolve and rarely did a straightforward answer satisfy the situations. But I stayed focused on trying to understand what was driving our opposing viewpoints, then negotiate and compromise from that point forward. It wasn't always easy, but I found my own successful pathway.

CHAPTER 15

The Accidental Entrepreneur

My department at Nationwide Entertainment Corp experienced major changes. My superiors wanted us to cut down on costs and improve efficiencies. They merged my organization with another one of my peers' because it would make things easier for our clients. My peer's group had most of the new process flows. My department merged with hers and my position was eliminated. I understood it was just business, but before I left, I did my best to ensure they took care of my team.

The day I walked out of the building for the last time in December 2010, it felt like a divorce. I loved working for the company, my job, and the people I worked with; I had great experiences there. I found it difficult to walk away from something I created. I had worked myself out of a job again because I had been so efficient at my duties.

It was a rough day. I had been through losing jobs before, but I wondered how many more times this would that happen to me? I wondered if I had been smart in continuously starting new departments and initiatives within a company. The nature of being a creator meant I never nurtured my baby and watched it grow up. I always had to look for a new baby to birth.

As I faced reality, I doubted myself. I lost confidence. I had built a solid career in 26 years. Even though I had broken down barriers by often being the only Black person or female in top IT and executive roles, times were changing. And I wasn't getting any younger. Would I get another chance to use my capabilities? All these thoughts flowed through my mind on that final day as I joined my sons for a basketball game that evening.

Whenever Harold traveled, I liked to do things with the boys. We loved bonding over basketball games. My babies were young men now; Arthur was 23 and Brandon was 16 years old. As we sat in the stands, Arthur and Brandon excitedly cheered for our team. I tried to be my usual self and act crazy with them, but I'm sure they realized something was wrong. After the game ended and we walked to the car, I contemplated whether to tell them now or later that I no longer worked at Nationwide Entertainment Corp.

As I drove down the highway, I broke the news to them.

"Mama, it's fine," Arthur said. "You will have a job in no time. You are good at what you do. Somebody will need your talents."

Arthur stunned me with his wisdom and encouragement! His words wiped out all the negative thoughts from earlier in the day. When I shared the news with Harold, he was very supportive too. He wouldn't let me sink back into depressing thoughts. He suggested I take the time to contemplate what I wanted to do and trust that everything would be fine. I felt so much gratitude for my amazing family!

I received a severance package, so I didn't need a new job immediately. I took a well-deserved break and explored my options. I spent the first month enjoying my family and traveling. Finding my next executive leadership role would take time. So, while I looked for that opportunity, I also kept my eyes open for any companies that needed my level of expertise but couldn't afford it. I didn't want to rest on my laurels. I planned to volunteer my time because I didn't want to let my skills get dull.

As it so happened, one of my previous employees was contracting at a firm. She invited me to come and help her with an initiative she was working on. I told her I would be happy to speak to the group.

The meeting went well, and I identified areas where I could help them. This company fit my criteria, so I offered to work for free. It was a minority-owned advertising agency. Although I didn't collect a paycheck, I would gain valuable experience into a side of business I always wanted to learn. The experience would only help me in my search for my next full-time role.

I learned their operations inside and out. As I worked on their challenges with the senior leadership team, they learned how to look at things differently. They also learned how to adjust their strategy and business model to capture more of the market share to increase their success. In hindsight, I drew on my experiences at this company on multiple occasions in years to come. So, my time invested here certainly paid off!

As the Spring and Summer months of 2011 continued to roll by, I continued volunteering with smaller companies, but didn't land a new full-time position. I asked myself what would I do if nothing came along? I contemplated something I had given little thought to previously: entrepreneurship. I know not everyone succeeds as an entrepreneur, so naturally, I wondered if I would.

A few of my family members were entrepreneurs, so I knew first hand it was hard work. Entrepreneurs work harder in their own business than when they worked for someone else. I also knew I would have to become a selling machine. You are never off duty! If I was going down this path, I needed to be strategic.

So, I did what I do well; I planned. With all the leadership training and education, I received, I needed to apply it to a new situation. I knew I needed to keep my skills strong, my relationships hot, and my mind sharp. Developing a strategic financial plan was necessary. It included continuing to volunteer for companies that would give me the opportunity to learn and grow in other areas. I planned on staying involved in my various professional groups by attending events of interest and things I enjoyed. I would continue to mentor others and apply for different positions.

During this time, I increased my networking. I knew that networking is just the starting point for building a relationship. Keeping this in mind, I had to determine how much time to invest in making new connections and nurturing them versus leveraging my existing relationships.

So, I applied a skill I learned early in my career. Every minute of your day should fit into your strategy. Here is what I mean by that. When you receive invitations to business functions, ask yourself some questions. Why am I going? Who do I need to meet and why? What do I plan to get from attending this event? Will I get a return on my investment of time?

Time is the most precious asset we have; once gone, we can't get it back. Besides, as an entrepreneur, you are the leader, doer and everything in between for your business. You don't have extra minutes in the day. None of us do, but it becomes real when you are on your own. So, I ran every event invitation through this strategic checklist. If it passed, then I attended the event. Networking helped keep me "in the know" about my industry.

Simultaneously, I read plenty and took many webinars to increase my level of knowledge regarding the latest challenges in technology and related industries. These activities kept my mind fresh and up to date. As for my financial plan, I took the time to examine my budget and determine how much money I needed to make. I looked at every expense and asked questions. Did we need this? Could we do it differently or cheaper? How can I maintain or increase how much I previously made and saved? How much longer could I afford to volunteer? I had a target date for when I needed to start my next paying opportunity.

I continued to plant seeds. I am a true believer in planting them everywhere, and the only ones that will grow are the ones meant for you. If you are faithful, sometimes you will plant in one area but reap a harvest someplace else. That is precisely what happened to me next.

One morning, I was at home, and my cell phone rang. It was one of my mentees from a previous company. I had not spoken to her in probably two years. She said she knew of a media company which I'll call Regional Broadcast Network. Their Atlanta division was looking for Chief Operating Officer and my mentee thought they could use my skills. I thanked her and told her I would investigate it.

I began my research. I discovered that the President of the company was an alumnus of Leadership Atlanta; so was I, just a part of a different class. I found my hook! I composed an email to her and started with our mutual connection. I then let her know I heard about their search and expressed my desire to learn more about the position. She responded with an invitation to have a conversation. It went extremely well. From there I passed several more rounds of interviews. At the end of this process, I received an offer. Unfortunately, the compensation package was not enough for it to be a mutually beneficial relationship.

But my newly formed entrepreneurial skills spotted an opportunity. I told them I knew it was hard for them to find the right executive candidate. Meanwhile, with the role unfilled, many business challenges remained unmet. I proposed that they hire me as a consultant to help them while they continued their search. I would also get them unquestionably prepared for the right COO. They agreed. I had landed my first client!

I started that engagement in October 2011. Our original agreement was for three months, but it stretched into 18 months, even after the new COO came on board. We made such significant progress, and I proved my value by helping them in other areas. Even though it wasn't my first time working in the broadcast media industry, I still learned a lot during this assignment.

With my first engagement launching me into entrepreneurship, I had to apply my skills to my business and work out my business model. Many benefits I had received as an employee I now had to provide myself. I thought about my health care needs for the first time in my working life. Thank God for Harold's job; I received coverage under his plan. I realized I alone had to make contributions into my retirement plan. And the only bonuses I would receive now was when I brought in more clients than projected.

Having control over my schedule meant I could take vacation and sick days whenever I wanted to; my "boss" would always approve. That was nice. But there was a downside to that freedom. I didn't get paid for those days. In fact, my new reality was if I didn't work, I didn't get paid. I had a lot to plan for in my business structure if I wanted to match and exceed the salary and benefits, I earned in the corporate world. If you are currently working for an employer, keep in mind that your benefits are not free. There is a price that your company is paying to invest in you and your colleagues. Working for myself gave me a newfound appreciation for this!

As I was working with Regional Broadcast Network, I knew the contract would eventually end. I had to land my next opportunity. I had to work and continue selling at the same time. I kept networking, attending events, and nurturing my relationships. One such conversation led to an opportunity for me to partner with another consulting firm. I would be a subcontractor. I thought it was a great fit. Their sales team found the clients, and I just needed to come in and perform my part of the work. No, I didn't get the lion's share of the profits, but I also didn't have the lion share of the headaches around securing the deal with the customer! We started on a short-term agreement that ended up going much longer. My income acquisition strategy was working out for the time being.

Right around this time, in 2013, my mother became ill. I was very concerned about the level of medical care she was receiving. I brought her to Atlanta to have her checked out by doctors I trusted. As an entrepreneur, I had total control over my time, so I had the flexibility to be an advocate for her; I didn't have to ask anyone's permission or worry if my job would be in jeopardy. I loved being able to focus on helping Mama without that worry. But the process of managing her appointments, going with her, providing care at home while still meeting my obligations on my assignments took its toll on me, but I did it.

Even as an entrepreneur, I found myself wearing my game face as I tried to let everyone around me think I was ok. I was exhausted, and I kept wondering if I would make it though. I finally had to trust and believe God didn't give me any more than I could handle. It sure was easier said than done though.

As I continued as a subcontractor for over a year, I knew I couldn't get comfortable. I knew firsthand that business changes happen. My partner company might not have another opportunity for me to work on. I had been taking on smaller contracts on my own while I worked for them. But I needed at least one significant engagement, so I could stay on track with my financial goals. So, I mapped out a strategy of things I could do on my own to keep moving forward.

I considered finding another partner firm first. My other course of action was to look at companies with open positions. Why was I looking for jobs that may or may not have been a fit for me? Well, I learned to view open positions as a sign that a company had a need and was in the process of change. There is a reason they are trying to fill that role. As I examined these opportunities, I would ask myself questions such as where does this company need help? Do I have anything to offer to help them move forward in the short term? If so, I formulated a pitch for them. This thinking kept me from getting discouraged if I didn't see a position that was an ideal fit for me.

My suspicions ultimately proved right, and the company I was subcontracting for did not have another opportunity for me at the end of the assignment. But fortunately, I already had my next engagement in the works. How it came about is a fascinating story.

Approximately two-and-a-half years prior when I was heavily in mentorship and networking mode, I connected with a woman I'll call Amanda. She had undertaken a massive company. She asked me for my insights and help with strategizing, since I was consulting with a partner company in the same industry. I willingly answered all her questions free of charge, and she was able to make a decision to move forward. I considered it a good seed sown and didn't think much of it after that.

Well, Amanda remembered. And now she was in need of a consultant to come in and help her organization through a major technology transformation initiative. Amanda had the authorization to hire a consultant. I asked Amanda what made her call me. She said, "I will never forget how you helped me when I needed guidance!" I was grateful that I had left such a positive impression. I was hired on as the consultant assisting her leadership team. We accomplished a lot during my 19-month stay. One of my goals was to work myself out of a job and help them transition all functions in-house. As usual, I met the objective. After the transition, I left the organization in May 2016.

Around this time, I came to a point in my business where I needed to refine my strategy again. I have been through this process over the years many times with past employers. Now it was time to put it into practice for myself. I examined my entrepreneurial trajectory to date. I started on my own with a single consulting contract. I gained traction. Then I partnered with established organizations and other entrepreneurs as a subcontractor. Then I took on my own engagements which had a strong focus on strategy, change management, and business technology transformation initiatives. Now I was asking myself the question how did I want my business to evolve? What changes did I need to make?

After much thought and consideration, I launched a new website (www.vickiwrighthamilton.com) and a new service. I added individual and organizational coaching to my business. I did so because it was something I was already doing. Every time I evaluated business strategies for a client, we always came around to examining the organization. I always helped them to determine if their structure was sound and if they had the right individuals for the new roles required to move forward. When leaders determined that one or more people on their team lacked skills, they wondered if they could sponsor training for these team members that would help them gain the skills they needed. I was already internally coaching the leadership team, and I have coached individuals through my mentorship experiences. I knew I could systematize some of the methodologies I used over and over to help more companies and individuals.

My entrepreneurial journey has certainly been worthwhile. But I would be dishonest if I only painted it as a rosy picture. If you are contemplating being a business owner at some point in your career, know that you will work harder than you ever have in your life. You are always "on," and always on the hunt for your next opportunity. If you have developed strong and genuine professional relationships, your network will be an incredible asset. It can help keep you in the midst of great decision makers and challenges you might be able to solve which others are facing within their companies.

You can't wait until you complete a project before you plant seeds for the next one. If you do, you can find yourself at a point where you are not making money while a sales cycle is going through completion. It can be tough waiting on your prospects to call you back, answer your emails, or approve your proposal; you have a sense of urgency because you are trying to get to your money, but they don't share your timeline. You must keep your game face on and avoid appearing too anxious or out of control. You must show patience and respect for their processes.

I have one final thought I would like to share regarding entrepreneurship. When you are working for a company as an employee, you become very involved. You belong to a team and you are vested in their mission. When you are consulting, you have to be involved and vested in the company's success, but it must be from a distance. You can't allow yourself to get too engrossed into the company because your engagement will ultimately come to an end. Leaving can be hard and make you feel very sad if you have not worked at a "comfortable distance." Knowing your boundaries will keep you agile and useful to the various companies you will serve.

CHAPTER 16

Caring for Family, Caring for Self

I began my story by sharing about my family, so it is where I will bring it to a close. For many of us, our parents are larger-than-life heroes to us when we are children. But as life goes on, the roles are reversed. Over the last few years, illness has been striking my family from multiple areas all at once. Although my husband and I had always taken care of some members of the family, the magnitude intensified. It all began with my mother back in 2013. Then Daddy took ill. Ultimately, we moved both my parents from St. Louis to Atlanta.

Juggling entrepreneurship and hands-on care for my parents was tough. Even with a flexible schedule, there was a limit to the workload I could handle if doctor and therapy appointments were taking chunks of time out of my week. As I mentioned before, if I didn't work, I didn't get paid. So, I had to be strategic about the projects I undertook. I also had to get help to augment my efforts, similar to when I used nannies, daycare centers, and babysitters when my kids were younger.

So, I gathered a team of professionals and my immediate family who pitched in to help lighten my load.

In 2014, a tragedy affected my family. We unexpectedly lost my beloved brother, Tommy. He meant the world to me but watching my parent's pain broke my heart. No parent should bury their child. For their sakes, I held my pain inside and tried to be strong for them. I figured that time and busyness would numb my pain.

I put on my coping game face and immersed myself in my work. I got so involved and took on as much as possible. At points, I didn't care if I charged for the hours or not. I kept moving 100 miles an hour to escape; stopping wasn't an option. If I stopped or slowed down, that would give me time to think. I didn't want to think at all. I didn't want to feel the pain of the most profound loss I had ever experienced in life. But I quickly learned that I couldn't bury my feelings forever. Something will happen or occur to bring them back up all over again.

The day came when I finally faced my pain and allowed myself to grieve. I was working on an important project for a client and I needed to be at my best. I had to clear my mind to apply myself effectively to the project. So, I went on my back deck that day and let myself cry. Tommy and I spent many wonderful times together on that deck. I took out pictures of him and set my thoughts free. I cried until I couldn't anymore. I wrote him a letter and expressed all my feelings.

Then something special happened. While I sat on the porch crying and writing, a red cardinal came and sat on the ledge. The bird instantly warmed my heart. One time, Tommy and I had a conversation about the afterlife. We tossed around our theories on how we would come back in our next life. Tommy said he would be a red cardinal. The bird landing on my ledge made me feel like Tommy was with me at that moment.

I talked to the bird as if it were Tommy. I told him how much I loved and missed him. When he flew away, my heaviness lifted. I noticed the sun shining. It was quite a lovely day. At that moment, I gave myself permission to take my coping game face off.

From that point on, I've been conscious about dealing with personal challenges because I can't perform at my best when issues are weighing me down. I have built a solid personal brand and professional reputation on follow through, a strong work ethic and quality. If I tarnish my reputation, it would taint my earning potential.

This brings me around to self-care. Since becoming an entrepreneur, I understand the value of time in new ways. I now value self-care, whereas I hadn't before. For years, I had given my all to my work and my family. As a mom and a wife, I took care of everyone first. I put myself last or, sometimes, not at all. When I worked corporate jobs, I didn't want my work responsibilities to overshadow being present for my sons. I attended all their sporting activities, and I was the one shuttling them to their doctor's and dentist's appointments.

But I didn't prioritize myself in the same way. I didn't create a strategic plan to nurture my aging body properly. How much did I need to increase my activity to stay healthy? Getting healthy was always part of the family's plan, and I knew it was 80% food and 20% exercise. But I wasn't careful about remembering to actually eat. So, my body held onto the food I gave it, as it thought I was starving it. I attended a workout class twice a week, but that wasn't enough activity for me.

Taking care of my aging parents has been a big eye-opener for me. I always saw them as vibrant, active, and very intelligent people. But their bodies and health changed right before my eyes. My vision for their golden years was for us to travel together and have great experiences together. But as I got ready to do more, they didn't feel like it. I realized too late that I had let some of the most precious years slip by. Now I appreciate just how valuable time is.

It has all come together for me. I am taking better care of myself physically and emotionally. I should have started younger, but I won't dwell on that. What is important is my commitment to my health today. I now add activities and appointments to my calendar that keeps my body strong, my mind sharp, and my emotions nourished. It has been the best gift I have ever given myself.

Through all my ups and downs, with a lot of hard work and consistency, my career as an entrepreneur has continued to excel. My family remains an essential foundation for me. I have learned to give myself the love and care I deserve. I have found the balance, perseverance, and strength to make it all work out. I have indeed been blessed.

Made in the USA
Columbia, SC
04 August 2021

42906302R00098